M000190502

1945   11   _____

Girl with Two Landscapes

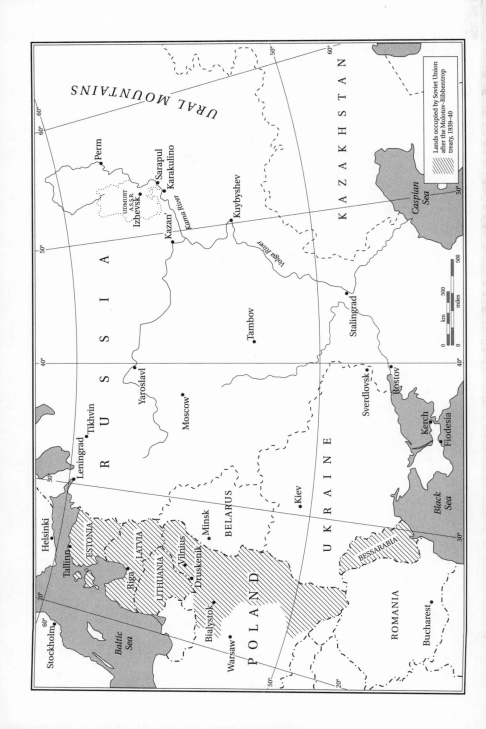

LENA JEDWAB ROZENBERG

Girl with Two Landscapes

The Wartime Diary of Lena Jedwab, 1941–1945

Translated by Solon Beinfeld
Foreword by Irena Klepfisz
Introduction by Jan T. Gross

HOLMES & MEIER
New York / London

Published in the United States of America 2002 by
Holmes & Meier Publishers, Inc.
160 Broadway • New York, NY 10038
www.holmesandmeier.com

Copyright © 2002 Dorothée Rozenberg

All rights reserved. No part of this book may be reproduced or transmitted in
any form or by any electronic or mechanical means now known or to be
invented, including photocopying, recording and information storage and
retrieval systems, without permission in writing from the publisher, except by
a reviewer who may quote brief passages in a review.

Originally published in Yiddish as *Fun heym tsu na-vanad: milkhome togbukh
1941–1945* in Paris, 1999.

This book has been printed on acid-free paper.

Designed by Brigid McCarthy

Library of Congress Cataloging-in-Publication Data

Rozenberg, Lena Jedwab, 1924–
    [Fun heym tsu na-vanad. English]
    Girl with two landscapes : the wartime diary of Lena Jedwab, 1941–1945 /
Lena Jedwab Rozenberg ; translated by Solon Beinfeld.
        p. cm.
    ISBN: 0-8419-1427-3 (cloth)
    1. Rozenberg, Lena Jedwab, 1924—Diaries. 2. Jews—Soviet Union—Diaries.
3. Jewish youth—Soviet Union—Diaries. 4. Jews, Polish—Soviet Union—
Diaries. 5. World War, 1939–1945—Jews—Soviet Union—Diaries. I. Title.

DS135.R95 R68 2002
940.53'089'924047—dc21

                                                        2002068864

Manufactured in the United States of America

FOR Sami, Flore, Doti
And their offspring

IN MEMORY OF
My mother, Freyde-Rive,
My father, Leyb,
My little brother, Moyshl,
And my sister, Sorele,
Who perished in the gas chambers of Treblinka

IN MEMORY OF my teachers and fellow students
Of the Yiddish school in Bialystok

Contents

Acknowledgments

I am most grateful to my father, Sholem Rozenberg, who preserved, transcribed, and published my mother's diary in the original Yiddish in Paris, helping to bring her back to her children and grandchildren at the very time when, day by day, we were losing her. He has truly performed a labor of love, and left us with a testimony to her literary and cultural identity.

Thanks to our friend Yosl Bergner, the renowned Israeli artist, for letting us use his painting *Girl With Two Landscapes* as cover art for this book. His picture, so evocative of the two landscapes of home and exile that are an undercurrent throughout the diary, has also been emblematic of our family throughout our lifetime: The original oil painting hangs in our parents' living room, and a lithograph of the same work graces the homes of each of their children.

I would like to thank Solon Beinfeld, Professor Emeritus of History at Washington University in St. Louis, for undertaking the translation of the diary from the original Yiddish into English. He helped give my mother an English voice, so that her story could be heard by non-Yiddish readers; and he made this effort even before publication of an American edition was assured. The role of the translator, so critical to understanding a text, is often underappreciated. Professor Beinfeld has succeeded not only in rendering my mother's words but in capturing the tone of her voice. I am also grateful for his historical research and footnotes that help place the diary entries in their proper context.

Thanks to Irena Klepfisz, Associate Professor of Women's Studies at Barnard College, and also poet, essayist and Yiddish translator, for her insightful Foreword and for her unwavering support throughout the diary project.

Thanks to Jan T. Gross, Professor of Politics and European Studies at New York University and author of *Neighbors: The Destruction of the Jewish Community in Jedwabne, Poland* (Princeton University Press, 2001), for providing a historical context to frame my mother's story.

Thanks to Miriam Holmes, for believing in the importance of my mother's personal and historical testimony, and to Sheila Friedling for her editorial wisdom.

Thanks to my husband, Michael Albert, for his constant support and help throughout this process.

DOROTHÉE ROZENBERG
Cambridge, Massachusetts
May 2002

Preface to the Yiddish Edition

A diary—a refuge in a world that is doomed.

The document that is being published here is the diary that Lena Jedwab, a Jewish girl from Bialystok, then sixteen years old, began to write in October 1941 in the children's home in the depths of the Soviet Union, where the tempest of war had stranded her. She kept this diary, with interruptions, until the end of the war.

In peacetime, the diaries of young people are no novelty: it is customary, during the adolescent years, for a boy or a girl to confide his or her intimate thoughts to this faithful written confidant. It helps the diarist to better grasp what is happening to his innermost self during a period of fundamental development. Sometimes individuals of a particularly inward-looking temperament keep diaries all their lives, eager for insight into their own complex feelings. Writers and artists are, of course, inclined toward this mode of introspection.

The diaries of people who happen to stand in the midst of extraordinary historical circumstances—and sometimes at their very culmination—belong to yet another genre. Their goal is to preserve a trace of the past, to fix the memory, to provide a chronicle for the future. The period of the Holocaust has left us a number of such documents, from which historians still draw valuable information about those dark years.

In Lena Jedwab's diary all three categories of this genre are combined. It is both an intimate witness to the pains and joys of ripening womanhood and a mirror of the soul of a sensitive, artistic personality. It is also—unintentionally—a chronicle, a description of a time and setting of particular historical interest. But above all, it is a tool, a means of saving herself, that the diarist used in order to maintain her mental clarity and emotional equilibrium at a time when catastrophic events had erased all the familiar signs by which a person normally locates his place in the world.

By means of her diary, Lena builds a nostalgic bridge of words to her distant home, perhaps already in ruins. It connects her to her parents, to her brother and sister, to friends—about whom she knows nothing—where and how they live, or even if they are alive at all. As someone who must daily redefine the contours of her being, she constructs over and over, with the patience of despair, the scenes of family life, the moments of vanished joy as well as images of her closest relationships.

But it is not only her own intimate circle that she thus symbolically rescues from disintegration, but also other basic elements of her identity. First and foremost is the language. Writing the diary in Yiddish is, to be sure, only natural for Lena. But she also uses it as a conscious means not to lose contact with a language that only yesterday filled every corner of her life, and from which she is now torn away just as surely as from her mother. Lena's struggle for her linguistic identity is no less moving than her desire for love, for recognition, and for happiness—desires that are evident on every page of her diary.

Whoever reads this document will certainly sense the burden of loneliness and wretched solitude that the writer bore and—with the help of this diary—overcame. But the reader will also be carried along by Lena's often-expressed drive toward life and creativity. He or she will understand how necessary it was for Lena to represent in her entries moods both of exaggerated dejection and of exaggerated pride. For these are the paths by which a sensitive, suffering person seeks a way out of her predicament.

At the same time one must marvel at Lena's ability to characterize people and circumstances succinctly and precisely. Though it may not have been her intent, the writer gives us sharp, subtle glimpses into the nature of "Soviet man" in those days. Her description and critical analysis of the Soviet village, among other scenes, are charming. Her means of expression may be somewhat naïve and overly emotional, but the sobriety of her judgments is striking.

Lena Jedwab's diary of the war years is thus a document that truly portrays a journey "from home to wandering."[*] Along the way, the author grasps at every day, every experience, as if to extract from it the meaning of her confusing reality. The success of this attempt can be measured in her poems (*Poems of Pain and Wandering* [Paris 1998]), which are like milestones in a reverse itinerary—this time, from wandering to the building of a new home.

YITZKHOK NIBORSKI
Professor of Yiddish
INALCO (Institut National des Langues et Civilisations Orientales)
Paris, France

---

[*] Translation of the Yiddish title.

Foreword

Irena Klepfisz

As readers we are drawn to diaries and journals because they provide us with an uncensored rendering of a person's thoughts and feelings. No other genre affords us the opportunity to glimpse the unmediated and unguarded intellectual and emotional landscape of another human being. Diaries recorded during periods of crisis make special claim on us as both scholars and lay readers, for it is through such writing that we can view history as present rather than past, as experience rather than honed and sifted narrative.

The personal narratives of Jewish experiences during World War II were initially perhaps an exception. Following the war, there were decades of Jewish silence, a silence imposed as much by the survivors' unwillingness to speak as a reluctance by others to listen. There are complex reasons why this occurred. Relevant to us now is that this silence has been broken, and in the past twenty years we have been witness to an outpouring of publication of Holocaust and Jewish memoirs. For obvious reasons, diaries and journals are far fewer in number. The most prominent and one of the earliest— perhaps the primary text of the Holocaust—is Anne Frank's *The Diary of a Young Girl*. (It is interesting that the recent controversy surrounding this text centers precisely on the question of the degree to which its uncensored writing was tampered with by some of its champions.) Anne's story is now familiar to millions: the years of hiding in "The Annex" in Amsterdam to avoid Nazi deportation, the family tensions, her relations with others, adolescence, love, and above all, reflections on the world into which she was born.

Through her youth and circumstances, Anne has come to represent—at least in popular American culture—the Jew as innocent, powerless victim, the artist who never had a chance to develop her talent.

Out of print for years (at least in the United States) are the diary and letters of another young woman, Hannah Senesh. A Hungarian teenager who eventually became an ardent Zionist and emigrated to Palestine, Hannah insisted on returning to Europe as a resistance fighter, where she was captured and executed by the Nazis. Her lack of recognition and popularity outside of Israel probably stems from the fact that unlike Anne's narrative, Hannah's could not be easily universalized (without her Zionist commitment it would make no sense), nor could it be promoted as one of female/Jewish victimhood. Despite her heroism, Hannah—who relinquished her safety—is not the girl protective Jewish parents automatically want their daughters to emulate.

Anne's and Hannah's diaries provide us with narratives of young women at the two extremes of Jewish experience between 1939 and 1945: passive resistance (by trying simply to survive) and active resistance (through exercising force). Clearly there are many other narratives whose experiences fall between these two, and we are fortunate that one of these has been preserved and is now available to both Yiddish and English readers: *Girl with Two Landscapes: The Wartime Diary of Lena Jedwab, 1941–1945.*

In order to begin to grasp the contribution that Lena's diary makes toward the literature of this period, it is important first to note some of the differences between Lena and the other two young women. Both Anne's and Hannah's roots are in Western Europe; their milieus are the middle-class, assimilated Jewish circles of Germany, Holland, and Hungary. As a result, their families encourage and are able to offer them a mainstream education. Anne's diary is written in Dutch; Hannah's diary and letters are mostly in Hungarian, though her later writings are also in Hebrew. Although they are not ashamed of being Jewish, both Anne and Hannah come to greater consciousness of their Jewishness as a result of the war and the persecution of Jews. For Hannah, the conversion to Zionism signals her overt acceptance of herself as a Jew. Finally, both—in very different ways—come under the control of the Nazis: Anne succumbs to typhus in Bergen-Belsen a few days before its liberation; Hannah is executed by a German firing squad while on a rescue mission.

Lena Jedwab is a very different girl, a different Jew, and she provides us with a narrative that hardly overlaps with those of Anne and Hannah. To begin with, her roots are in Eastern Europe; her native city is Bialystok, then part of Poland, where she is born into an extremely poor family. When she begins keeping her journal in 1941, she is fluent in Polish and almost so in Russian; yet she writes her diary in her native Yiddish, a language to which she has a strong emotional attachment and political commitment. Her Jewish identity—rooted in secular Yiddish culture—is thus not only a given, but something she wants to protect and guard against assimilation. In addition, the abject poverty of her family would have precluded any higher education; at one point she and her sister are sent to a special boarding school because her parents cannot afford to feed them at home. Later, she attends a Yiddish *gymnazium*, which is very rare for a girl from such a poor family. Like Anne and Hannah, she is an exceptionally gifted student. Unlike them, her education is also infused with a Marxist and socialist vision and a keen sense of political responsibility and purpose.

There are other major differences in Lena's circumstances that make her diary an invaluable document that broadens our knowledge of Jewish experiences during the war. Her journal covers the years between 1941 and 1945 in the Soviet Union. During this time, unlike Anne and Hannah, Lena is on her own, without parents to comfort her or against whom she can rebel. From the age of sixteen, when she is stranded in a summer camp for young Communist Pioneers, and for the next four years, Lena has no adults who love her and whom she can trust for daily advice or guidance in making life-changing decisions. Also, she never comes into direct contact with the Germans, following the war and the fate of the Jews of Bialystok through news reports and personal accounts of those with whom she comes in contact. At no time isolated specifically for her Jewishness (though she encounters enough anti-Semitism for a lifetime), she remains a "civilian" in a war-torn, collapsing, starving country, who—without any role models—must figure out a way to grow up and make herself self-sufficient. And she survives—together with her diary.

But even without these comparisons, there are numerous aspects of the diary that demand our attention, admiration, and affection for its author and her writing. First and foremost is Lena's intelligence and literary talent. Lena is a conscious writer. By that I mean that she is aware of the power of language and of the written word. At the age of sixteen, when the journal begins, she is trilingual, fluent in Polish and Yiddish and well on the way in Russian. From the beginning, her love of literature—and the theater—and her linguistic abilities are evidenced throughout her diary entries in the descriptions of her physical surroundings, whether the beauty of nature or the harsh conditions of her room; of the people with whom she comes into contact; and of her own feelings and thoughts. Throughout, she repeatedly refers to and cites from the works of major European writers such as Gorky, Tolstoy, Mickiewicz, Mayakowski, Turgenev, and Heine; and she seems as comfortable citing Psalm 137 in Polish as Heine's poetry in German. It is sometimes easy to forget that she is only a high school student. Her literary and linguistic talents are indeed astonishing.

Yet despite her European literary sophistication, it is the Yiddish language to which she gives the most thought and it is Yiddish that she commits herself to preserving. Yiddish is her mother's tongue and embodies her emotional connection to Jewish life and the Bialystok home she has lost. Where, she wonders, will she be able to find Yiddish books again? Writing her journal in Yiddish, encouraging other children and peers to continue speaking the language—despite the prohibition of the home's Jewish director (he thinks they'll never learn Russian if they continue speaking it)—represent her attempts to keep alive her Jewish roots and her Yiddish-speaking culture. At one point, when she comes across a story by the Yiddish writer I. L. Peretz in Russian, she translates it back as she goes along and "reads" it to the others in the original Yiddish.

So important is this language, this intimate connection to her Jewishness, that quite early in the diary Lena admits to feeling shame because she finds herself, not unnaturally, beginning to think in Russian. She understands, instinctively, the fragility of Yiddish—of any language for that matter—when not nurtured by daily use. And she understands the dependence of her own secular Jewish identity on Yiddish culture. When she leaves the children's home and moves to Moscow, she records that she has begun a story in Russian because there is no one to write for in Yiddish. Still, she doesn't give up the dream and makes plans to try to connect with the great actor and director Solomon Mikhoels and his Yiddish theater. And one of the last diary entries describes a visit to her friend's home in the Ukrainian town of Niezhin and her delight in encountering a Yiddish cultural group, who unfortunately admire her Yiddish "because few young people of my age now can speak like me or even know Yiddish literature."

Lena's interests are remarkably broad, and she is an ardent student who in her journal sometimes takes on the role of an adult or teacher, admonishing herself when she doesn't keep up with her studies or receives a grade lower than "excellent." Realizing that she cannot stay in the children's home forever, she decides to go to Moscow to study engineering. To do that, however, she must "skip" a year and meet course requirements for the tenth grade: these include physics, algebra, geometry, trigonometry, chemistry, German, literature, and history. She is, it is clear, exceptionally bright, but it is her determination and self-discipline, not her intelligence alone, that pull her through. With no one but herself to urge her on, the eighteen-year-old finally is accepted by Moscow's Bauman Technical Institute. Given the difficult circumstances at the children's home— her isolation, hunger, emotional instability during war, lack of guidance—Lena's achievement is remarkable indeed.

But Lena is not a machine. There are moments when she, like any teenager, must play hooky. Instead of getting up at four in the morning to cram, she finds "a better way":

I spent a whole day on the other bank of the Kama. I picked flowers and red berries, bathed! I didn't think about studying at all. Someone might call it a case of lightheadedness! But the weather is so beautiful, the sky light blue, the Kama cool. The boat rocks lightly in the water and I see a lovely spot, then golden stalks, a young walnut grove, bunches of flowers, and an abundance of juicy, red berries. Summer—the loveliest time of the year! A pity that I can't often spend time in such a palace of nature. It's so pleasant to be here now! Harebrained hothead, weak-willed creature, enough carrying on about the weather! You're satisfied, it's enough. Time to get busy with exams!

This entry is typical of the character and richness of the diary—Lena's awareness and detailed description of her surroundings, her responsiveness to and engagement with nature, her ability to appreciate and immerse herself in what is good at the moment, and her ability to parent herself by alternately allowing for indulgence and then imposing discipline.

Lena does get to Moscow not only because she meets the course requirements, but because she works and earns money for her upkeep. But once there, she finds no break in her physical and emotional hardships. In the children's home, she lost and broke her glasses, succumbed to various illnesses, suffered hunger. In Moscow, she never has enough money or food and finds schoolwork more difficult than before (she abandons engineering and goes on to the university). Though surrounded by acquaintances, she is constantly lonely and, in the most cruel twist of circumstance, she is seriously hurt in a tram accident.

But Lena insists and overcomes and moves toward adulthood. In the children's home, as a budding adolescent, she first begins to long for romantic involvements. Initially, though her body yearns for contact, she feels only disappointment in herself and in the boys around her when she feels sexually aroused but romantically alienated. "I like Volodya's external appearance, but I am repelled by his inner nature," she writes. It is only later in Moscow that she experiences her first love affair with the son of a former teacher and is forced to sort through, again by herself, the intricacies of her feelings.

In this most intimate area—sexuality—Lena seems more starkly alone, unable to trust anyone to help her understand herself and others. For example, she is aware at the home of a teacher's involvement with a nineteen-year-old girl and suspects that the director is having relations with some of the young women. This is, in part, confirmed when she secretly reads the Polish journal of another girl. (Later that day, she acts out her guilt over this transgression by breaking her glasses.) Our awareness today of the frequency of such abuse between older men and vulnerable girls, especially teenagers, enables us to fill in the gaps. But Lena cannot. She is a product of a socialist education and never considers her gender as limiting or her sex as frail. She dreams freely and sets her goals—whether in her studies or her physical work—an attitude totally in conformity with Marxist principles and Soviet policies toward women. However, she gives no hint in the diary of having been presented with an analysis of sexual politics. As a result, she remains most naïve in this area. And it is remarkable that she is able to teach and protect herself to the degree that she does.

I have stressed the absence of comforting, loving adults in Lena's life because I think it is one of the major themes of the journal and perhaps, because of her achievements, one easily overlooked. In fact, Lena refers to it frequently. During the years in which she keeps the journal, she is constantly searching for someone on whom she can rely, sometimes turning to teachers, at other times to the parents of friends; and throughout she has recurrent dreams of her mother, which re-create reunion, separation, and death in a variety of forms. For all her protestation about independence and self-reliance, she longs for the dependence that was permanently left behind in Bialystok and that she never finds again.

That she manages to survive physically, despite this enormous absence, is wonder enough. But the way she survives is perhaps even more remarkable. For Lena's journal is not only a record of external hardships and personal emotional struggles, it is a document of moral struggles as well. In almost all instances, especially during her years at the home in Karakulino, Lena's moral responses to her circumstances and her sensitivity to the complexities of her situation are shaped by her Marxist education. Lena is always grounded politically and socially—conscious of hierarchies, of the potential for abuse of power, and committed to the principle of fairness. Despite the extreme physical deprivations at the home, she participates in and organizes—well everything—academic discussions, theater productions, literary programs, the children's governing council, the local Young Communist organization, surprise birthday parties, holiday celebrations. Popular with other children (she is elected head of the council as well as the Communist group), she nevertheless must learn to negotiate a narrow path between her position as an academic and performance "star" and group leader (and therefore the object of envy) and her place as one of the people. Her awareness of her relationship to others enables her to achieve this balancing act amazingly well. She acquires many friends, and inevitably also some detractors. Among the latter is the director of the home with whom she has ongoing problems and sometimes clashes over issues of principle.

But for all the sophistication of her class analysis—she systematically documents the background, political commitment, and intellectual achievements of the students and adults around her—we are repeatedly reminded of her youth and inexperience. And it is this ongoing contrast between her naïveté and her worldliness that gives the journal much of its moral weight and poignancy. Lena herself is frequently uncomfortably aware of the discrepancies between her feelings and her socialist upbringing and between her education and the reality she encounters. For example, the peasants she meets when she works as a fuel supplier for agricultural machinery and to whose struggle she has been for years theoretically committed repel her, for the most part, by their anti-Semitism and crudeness. The eighteen-year-old Lena scolds herself for her reactions, but we have to admire her for not hiding them or trying to rationalize them. Even more admirable, given the degree to which they do mistreat her, is her ability to remind herself of what she has been taught and still believes to be true: the peasants have nothing and their prejudices are not innate but learned. Here is Lena "correcting" her attitude toward her co-workers after they've stolen her food, thrown mud at her, and cursed her for her Jewishness. "Sometimes I accuse the tractor drivers of being coarse, crude, cruel. Yes, that's all true. But is it not possible to find the reasons that cause it? Is it really their fault? How could they be polite and good-natured when their lives are so hard and cruel?" That Lena can remember and hold on to this understanding despite her experiences embodies the specialness of her character and the strength of her socialist education.

Also moving is her ability to admit to the differences between the other workers and herself without leaping to a sense of superiority. She feels the intellectual chasm that exists between them, yet she also recognizes their strengths. When one of the workers is badly injured, she is stunned to see him working the next day. She realizes that for him there is no choice: his family needs the money. She goes on to make the following comparison: ". . . how many days and weeks would I, or some other 'big-city intellectual,' have been sick in bed and taken medicine?. . . when I consider these circumstances, I forgive them everything. Forgive them even for persecuting me as a Jew. . . . I am more and more convinced of how complicated life is and how false was the way I imagined it in my fantasy. Only now do I begin to recognize it." Moreover, her education and strong Marxist beliefs do not prevent her from seeing the miserable conditions in which the peasants live and from asking, "Where is the 'merry, happy collective-farm life'?"

Lena's moral concerns, usually expressed through socialist principles, always play a part in determining her behavior toward and her judgments of others. When daily rations at the children's home frequently consisted of only a few grams of bread or watery soup, power struggles predictably manifested themselves through food distribution. Lena observes how the cook and group leaders often give themselves and their favorites more food than the official ration. In the diary, she expresses both anger and puzzlement over those who participate in such practices and refuses to ally herself with any individual just for the sake of obtaining more food. Indeed, she and some other student leaders sometimes refuse extra portions because it would be unfair to the other children.

Yet, for all her moral perceptions, Lena does not recognize the implications of her own attachments, including her acceptance of invitations by certain teachers who give her treats in their quarters, as possibly the same strategy for survival—manifested more indirectly—that others use more blatantly. This lack of awareness is evidenced by her lack of embarrassment in conveying the details of these episodes in the diary entries and her puzzlement over the envy of others. As a result, she dwells unselfconsciously on the pleasure she derives from being singled out by an adult as worthy of attention and affection, rather than on the rewards that such an association can bring. In looking for emotional nurturance, she willingly accepts material support, though even that is only momentary.

In reading these entries, however, we never feel that Lena is being hypocritical. For me, one of the diary's most significant aspects lies in watching Lena work out moral issues and dilemmas. The fact that this adolescent devotes such an enormous amount of emotional and intellectual energy in sifting through moral questions makes the diary an invaluable document of human struggle in times of extreme distress. Repeatedly we are reminded that Lena is a girl trying to leap from the adolescent world of contemplating theory into the adult world of action and consequences, and that she is trying to do so without any sympathetic guide. Maturity and sixty years of hindsight enable us to know what Lena at eighteen in the 1940s does not: that moral purity is almost impossible to maintain. Compromises are inevitable, and, as readers, we never condemn her precisely because Lena *is* so morally focused and because she is always so vigilant that her behavior not deteriorate into a struggle solely focused on survival.

As reflected in her journal, Lena has grace, wit, enormous intelligence, and an astonishing enthusiasm and thirst for education and for finding beauty in nature and art. She is a thoroughly social

individual who yearns and actively searches for permanent attachments and affection. She is also a writer who seeks the solitude of
her journal to express the pain of overwhelming loss and hardship
brought on by the war around her. Her gift in evoking these sometimes contradictory aspects of her own personality, in revealing
details of the hardships endured by many Jews and Russians, and in
persistently articulating her moral and Marxist consciousness
make Lena's journal a literary treasure. It should be read alongside
the writings of Anne Frank and Hannah Senesh for a deeper, more
complex view of the experience of Jewish youth during World War II
and for a more nuanced understanding of individual suffering and
willed achievement.

Introduction

Jan T. Gross

In September 1939, Poland was attacked and occupied by two of its neighbors—Hitler's Germany and Stalin's Russia. The Wehrmacht crossed into Poland from the west on September 1, and the Red Army from the east on September 17. Nazi Germany and Soviet Russia thus found themselves in tacit collaboration for the next twenty months, and as a result, the eastern half of Poland's prewar territory was incorporated into the Soviet Union. It was in that half, in the town of Bialystok, that Lena Jedwab and her family lived until the summer of 1941, when Hitler unexpectedly attacked the Soviet Union.

Under the Soviet regime in the territories newly incorporated into the USSR, Polish Jews fared as well, or as poorly, as everybody else. They were subject to the very same measures of sovietization as the rest of the population, but they had a somewhat different perspective to evaluate the experience: in September 1939 in eastern Poland, Soviet occupation stemmed the takeover by German troops and the establishment of Nazi rule. The Germans invaded Bialystok on September 15, 1939; but barely a week later, on September 22, they were replaced by the Soviets. The Jews of Bialystok welcomed the Red Army, which they saw as the lesser of two evils. Being subject to Soviet or Nazi rule were the only alternatives; and the Jews had a clear awareness of what might have happened had the Soviets not arrived, because they had already been brutalized by the invading Germans.

To justify its invasion of Poland in September 1939, the Soviet government announced that it was compelled to enter Polish territory in order to protect the interests of national minorities, specifically those of the Ukrainians and the Byelorussians. This pretense at national liberation was, of course, but a fig leaf used to cover Soviet imperial ambitions. Yet initial Soviet policies (replacement of the Polish state administration with locally recruited volunteers, for instance) as well as a variety of steps taken to follow up on the promise of national liberation (promotion of local languages in schools, or encouragement of Yiddish theater, for example) created a general atmosphere of ethnic emancipation. People belonging to ethnic minorities—and one should be mindful that these so-called minorities were a significant majority in Soviet-occupied territories—initially lost the humiliating sense of being second-class citizens.

In the experience of the Jewish community, a confusing paradox was associated with the process of sovietization. In short order, following the Soviet annexation of this area, Jewish community life as well as a dense network of prewar cultural and political institutions were destroyed, political parties were banned, and the Zionist movement forced underground; secularization was imposed on the Jews, tens of thousands of Jews were forcibly deported into the Soviet interior, and leading citizens from all walks of life were arrested. And yet the Jewish collective memory of Soviet rule is not unequivocally negative. Why, then, would any Jews have any illusions about what the Soviet regime had in store for them?

They did, I believe, because the Soviet approach to so-called nationality problems was unusual. According to the traditional pattern of discrimination, familiar to national minorities, as long as such groups kept to themselves they were tolerated. Only when the process of social change led segments of the minority population out of their self-imposed isolation, or when they actively sought assimilation, would the dominant nationality be provoked to show anger, contempt, and frequently violence. The opposite was true under the Soviet regime: here Jewish insularity, willful Jewish separation from the rest of society, was not tolerated. Jews could acquire Soviet citizenship, with all the rights and entitlements that went with that honor, but they could no longer sustain their community life. They were given "equality" with everybody else as

Soviet citizens; but as they promptly discovered, this meant only that, along with everybody else, they were equally deprived of all rights. And, as a result, they could not organize their lives simultaneously as a distinct Jewish community *and* as citizens of the state that had jurisdiction over them.

But this reversal of the traditional pattern of discrimination was disorienting, and initially scores of people, especially young people, grew to appreciate the "nationality policies" of the Soviet regime. Yiddish schools, for example, were allowed to continue, although they became a tool for sovietization. The Jewish population took advantage of the educational system, which particularly benefited children from poor families, giving them greater access to education. Lena is a good example of the younger Jewish generation that embraced the new Soviet regime, eagerly joining the Pioneers (the official Communist youth organization); however, in her case, she did so without losing her strong sense of Jewish identity.

Lena was a teenager when the Germans unexpectedly attacked the Soviet Union on June 22, 1941, breaking the German-Soviet Non-Aggression Treaty that had paved the way for the partition of Poland. Lena was a camp counselor in a Pioneer summer camp in the Lithuanian health resort of Druskenik. The German attack was broadcast to a stunned Soviet audience by Soviet foreign minister Molotov, denouncing Hitler's betrayal of Stalin. (The short story that forms the prologue to Lena's diary mentions the Molotov address.) The camp administrators tried to bring the children back to Bialystok, but were unable to do so because the railway bridge to Grodno (along the route back) had been destroyed. Instead, they evacuated the children deeper into the Soviet Union: first to Sarapul, then eventually to a "childrens' home" (or orphanage) in Karakulino, in the Autonomous Soviet Republic of Udmurtia. There, children from the summer camp joined refugee children from other Soviet territories. Many Polish children thus ended up, like Lena, in Soviet schools and orphanages during the war.

Lena would never see her family again. During her subsequent peregrinations in the Soviet interior she kept a diary, which—as readers will soon discover—is written with an exceptional literary talent and freshness of insight. She leaves in it important testimony, not only illustrating the personal and psychological development of a young woman but also telling us much about the lives of young refugees within a number of Soviet institutions, among them an orphanage, a collective farm, and Moscow University.

Separated from her family by the vagaries of war, she nevertheless suspects the horrible fate that befell them under the Nazi occupation. Although she was not to learn the truth until much later, the Nazis entered Bialystok on June 27, 1941, a few weeks after Lena left. They established the Bialystok ghetto in August 1941. Several waves of mass deportations to extermination camps followed, primarily to Treblinka but also to Auschwitz and Majdanek. The first liquidation of the ghetto was launched in February 1943, and the final liquidation, which met with fierce resistance from the Jewish underground, in August 1943. Lena's family perished in Treblinka.

Like many other Jews all over the world, Lena was a helpless, distant witness to the tragedy of her people and her loved ones. We are all grateful for her testimony.

Girl with Two Landscapes

Lena, circa 1943

*This short story is a work of semiautobiographical
historical fiction that sets the stage for the diary that follows. Lena started
working on it in September 1942 (see entry for the fourteenth of October,
1942), and completed it in Moscow around 1945.*

Mirl: A Story

*S*he dreamed of her mother. A tiny mother with a pair of hazel
eyes, one of which tears even when she is smiling. With her small
but broad hands Mama kneads the dough for the *milchig** cake
and looks at the clock every few minutes, afraid she might be late.
Mama's hands hurry around the big blue bowl, with its raw, fresh
dough, and Mirl can already feel the taste of the hot butter cookies
that will emerge from it. Oh, her mother is a master of butter pastry.
And not just butter pastry. . . . She is an expert at everything! Pa
tells her that every time she sets the table, and she smiles shyly and
wipes her left eye with her handkerchief. Today Mama is trying
harder than usual and tastes the dough several times, as if to persuade herself that nothing is missing: enough salt, enough eggs,
cream, and sugar. Mirl knows that Mama is going to all this trouble
for her, and she is very proud of that. How good Mama is! The last
few days she's been busy preparing Mirl for her departure to the
sanatorium: washing, ironing, packing. Now she's preparing
baked goods for the trip. And although the travel time is no more
than four or five hours—and at night at that—she has mixed
enough dough for pastry to last a whole week. That's how Mama
is—she likes abundance. When Mirl is having a dress made, she
stands near the seamstress and asks her three times to leave a wide
hem: "A child grows."

---

* Under Jewish law, meat and milk products must not be consumed together. Foods are
therefore often categorized as *fleyshig* (containing meat) or *milchig* (dairy).

Mirl opens her valise, which stands ready, and examines her "possessions." On top lie a pair of thin cotton dresses, made for her recently; underneath, the white satin blouse, the cherry-colored jacket, then the maroon woolen sweater, the red cloth dress. "A mother is still a mother," she thinks, quietly pulling the cloth dress out of the valise and slipping unnoticed to the wardrobe to hang it up. Who needs both a cloth dress and a woolen sweater in summertime? In case of bad weather, the sweater will do by itself. But why start up with Mama? If she notices, she'll worry. Why cause her heartache? Quietly closing the wardrobe, she glances at her mother again—did she see, or not? No. Mama paid no attention because she's too busy at the oven and preoccupied.

Here come all her friends, girls and boys, to say good-bye. Round little Sorele, always laughing; Mashe with her long black braids, short Moyshl, and Zavl tall and thin. . . .

The room is filled with the loud sounds of children's voices, Sorele's laughter ringing above the rest. Finally it's time to say good-bye. Everyone wants to go to the station. Even Mirl's younger sister, ten-year-old Adaska, doesn't want to be left out. Mirl feels a bit lost. Such a fuss! She's also afraid that her mother will suddenly start to cry, as she usually does when saying good-bye. To tell the truth, she has a heavy heart herself. She's never gone away by herself before. Now she's going away for the whole summer to a sanatorium, where all the children will be strangers and all her friends will be far away. All the same, it will be interesting to see what the sanatorium looks like, and she wishes she were there already.

Mirl screws up her courage and suggests to her mother that they say good-bye on the spot. That way, Mama won't have to go to the station for no reason. Papa has come home tired from work, and his supper has to be prepared. The gang will accompany her and everything will be fine. It's hard to convince Mama that Mirl can leave without her, that no calamity will happen. Mirl must use her argument of last resort: she reminds her mother that she is a grown-up, that she's recently turned fifteen, that she can be relied on completely. The gang supports her, taking on itself full responsibility for her successful departure. Mama smiles and allows herself to be persuaded. At the same time she blinks hard, first with her left eye, then with the right. She suppresses the tears that gather in the corners of her eyes. Mirl is very troubled and feels like crying, but she is ashamed: after all, she is a grown-up! Like an adult, she shakes Papa's hand and then Mama's. As if to convince herself and also her mother that there's no reason to cry, she says confidently: "We'll see each other soon. I won't be gone forever, after all. Two months will fly by quickly." Mama smiles and wipes her eyes. Adaska stands next to her. To hide her agitation she undoes the ribbon in Adaska's braid and then braids her hair again. When Moyshl takes Mirl's suitcase and heads for the door, and everybody follows him out, Mama accompanies the whole gang to the courtyard. At the last minute, Mirl can't stand it any longer and rushes into her arms. But fearing that she might burst into tears, she pulls back and looks her mother in the eyes. Her mother's eyes glisten moistly as she strokes Mirl's head. "You mustn't cry, silly, you're a grown-up."

Mirl has to hurry to catch up with the gang, who have gone on ahead. For a while, she feels her mother's gaze behind her, filling her with a loving warmth that flows through her whole body. She is already on Tenth Street, close to the station, and she still can see her mother's moist eyes, gazing at her lovingly. "Mama, dear, beloved Mama," Mirl wants to say to her, but she cannot. Her voice is stuck in her throat, and she can only move her lips. But her mother cannot hear her, and Mirl tries with all her might—Ma. Suddenly she hears her own voice—and opens her eyes.

She has to close them again at once, blinded by a bright ray of sunlight. She sees her mother again, but not for long. Her mother has disappeared. Everything has disappeared. Vestiges of thoughts. Emptiness. She tries to collect her thoughts, but she doesn't succeed. She opens her eyes again. This time she shields them from the bright light with her hand. Where is she anyway?

A big sunny room with many beds, as in a hospital. She remembers: yes, of course, she is in the sanatorium. Gradually all her thoughts come back to her. Now she's awake. In the room it is quiet. The only sound is the regular breathing of six sleeping children. Her neighbor, the blond Russian girl, smiles in her sleep; she must be dreaming of something pleasant. Mirl observes her. She is pretty, this Valya. Her skin is golden brown and glowing; her hair, pale blond. In front, her hair is almost white from the sun. Mirl likes her, though she doesn't show it. Valya knows a lot of songs. She knows all the rules of the Pioneer[*] camp, since this is not her first time there. She is captain of the *Otryad*, the detachment of Young Pioneers, and all obey her commands. Now, asleep, she is smiling.

Mirl doesn't want to sleep anymore. The room is sunny and light. The hoarse crowing of roosters wafts in through the open window. It is still early. Mirl recalls her dream. Her mother is probably still asleep. No, not at all. Her mother rises very early. She's probably making breakfast for Papa—he leaves for work early. What day is it today? It must be Sunday. Today isn't a working day. It's a visiting day for parents. Maybe her mother will come? The thought cheers Mirl up. Sunday is a good day! She's in a good mood, and stretches out the length of the bed. The sun shines widely through the open windows and lures her outdoors, into the fresh, open air. Mirl throws off her blanket and lowers her feet into her slippers. She slips her flowered robe on her bare shoulders and quietly steals out of the room so as not to wake her sleeping comrades.

Mirl breathes deeply in the fresh morning air, which tickles her nostrils, making them tremble lightly. Total silence reigns. All three buildings of the sanatorium are sunk in deep sleep. The tall trees stretch their branches majestically toward the sun. A light breeze sways in the leaves, lulling them into a sweet dream. "It will be a beautiful day," thinks Mirl, lifting her head to the clear blue sky. "Not one cloud!" Dreamily she steps on the soft grass, damp from the dew, not knowing herself where she's going. Nearby the Niemen snakes along, glistening in the sun like a silver ribbon. Mirl doesn't feel her feet carrying her to the river. Carefully she removes a shoe and sticks one foot into the water. *Brrr* . . . the water is still cold. She turns back. They'll probably go swimming about twelve o'clock, after the late-morning snack. Now she'll go back. What can

[*] Pioneers: Soviet youth organization.

she do here by herself? Suddenly she hears a faint sound. She looks around: nobody there. The sound seems to come from above. Undoubtedly it's a plane. "Somebody else isn't sleeping," she thinks. "The pilot's already taking his practice flights. He must be quite a fellow!" She's often seen the pilots doing loops, swinging back and forth in the sky, and she is really in awe of them. That's quite a feat! A person flying like a bird, but even faster than a bird. And when he appears in the sky with his steel wings, he frightens away all the winged creatures.

But where is that airplane? The noise grows stronger and comes even closer. It surely isn't one plane, but a group. Mirl cranes her neck and looks up to the sky, searching with eager eyes. The buzzing grows stronger, and suddenly several planes appear on the horizon, forming a triangle in the air. Their movement is slow and heavy. Mirl waits in vain for them to perform their tricks. "The pilots must still be drowsy," she thinks. "They must have just gotten up." With her neck craned and eager eyes she follows the group now emerging. She recognizes a bomber among them, like the one Moyshl pointed out to her in the May Day parade. Then, too, the planes flew in the same formation, and Moyshl explained to her that the group was made up of a bomber and the fighter planes that surround and protect it in battle. Where are they flying to now? Before she can think of an answer, another group appears, and parallel to it yet another. The groups of planes once again form a triangle and fly, silent and heavily, in the same direction. "Today there are definitely maneuvers," Mirl decides, and follows the formation with her eyes.

Suddenly it seems to her that she can see a black swastika on one of the planes. A grain of uneasiness steals into her heart. It cannot be. She must be mistaken. They're flying very high, and she must have gotten it wrong. What business have German planes to be over Soviet soil? And so early? And most important, who would let them into the country? She stares at the sky for a long time, until the formation disappears from the horizon. She shakes off the bad thoughts and decides that she made a mistake. Slowly she returns to the dormitory and lies down. Turning her face to the blank wall—so the sun won't interfere with her sleeping—she closes her eyes. Dozing, she still pictures the formation, and sees quite clearly a black swastika flying, slow and heavy across the clear blue sky.

Three times the bugle sounded. Children peel out of every bed, and open their sleepy eyes. There's no time to dawdle in bed: they have to hurry outside for morning gymnastics. Swiftly they spring up from under the covers and hastily make their beds. Five minutes to comb your hair and put on your gymsuit: black shorts and a white athletic shirt. So you have to hurry up. The bugle sounds again. Youngsters file out of every room and quickly fall into rows outside. The senior Pioneer leader calls out: "Attention!" Her commands are sharp and regular, and the children's arms and legs swing rhythmically to the beat. Hands entwined over the head, the torso leans to the right and the left, and it looks like a young forest bending its branches, moved by the wind. "One!" A forest of hands is raised toward the sky. "Two!" Left legs are raised gently and bent deeply at the knee. "Three!" Arms gracefully slice through the air, forming two right angles from top to bottom and to the sides. In tandem the body leans forward, stretching the left leg backward. The slim young bodies form a swarm of birds. For a second, it seems that, any moment now, they'll tear the other foot from the ground and lift off into the air. "Four!" They return to the starting position.

The command is repeated several times. It exercises all the muscles, which seem to hum with joie de vivre. Oh, happy, carefree childhood! These children are the future masters of the world, it seems, who will inherit all its treasures, all their parents' knowledge. It is they who will rule the earth, the waters, and the heavens, they who are destined to enjoy the pleasures of free, creative work. Now they're still young. The nation sees to it that they are free to develop physically and intellectually. A network of Pioneer camps and sanatoriums spreads out throughout the land, where children can rest after the school year, gain new strength, and harden their young bodies.

Morning gymnastics has ended. In a minute the children scatter in every direction. They skip along, hurrying to wash up. The cold water is bracing and cools their overheated bodies. They splash each other, stopping up the faucet with a finger so that the stream of water lands on a kid nearby. That kid does the same in turn, and so starts the morning commotion, a mix of children's laughter, shouting, and the first songs of the day.

Things are especially lively in the boys' washroom. At two neighboring faucets stand Vladek and Avreml, the biggest pranksters in the whole sanatorium. As Avreml washes himself diligently on the chest, neck, and face, until the soap gets into his eyes, Vladek seizes him by the back of the neck and sticks his head under the faucet, which he has turned on to maximum force. The water snakes down Avreml's hair, neck, and face. Avreml gulps and gasps for breath. With soapy hands he seeks out the guilty party, grabbing the firm hand that is holding the back of his neck, and holds on to it till he frees his head. Now he'll take his revenge! With one finger he turns the stream of water on Vladek, who jumps away, but to no avail. He's left standing like a wet hen, holding on to the gym shorts that cling to his bare skin. The boys gathered around them laugh at the joke and forgive Avreml, who has sprayed quite a few of them.

Vladek is planning a new prank when, all of a sudden, who should appear but Grisha, the Pioneer leader, and the washroom grows still. Grisha is a nineteen-year-old blond youth with a genial face and childlike merry eyes that reveal that he, too, is a good prankster who can give as good as he gets. But now he pulls on a mask of seriousness and is angry with his boys. They respect Grisha. He's the idol of all the older boys. Who can swim like him? And lift heavy weights with one hand? And play chess? And shoot a rifle? Every time the boys have target practice at the white board with the black circles, they envy their troop leader. All he has to do is close one eye and pull the trigger and a hole appears in a black circle. It's not for nothing that Grisha wears the insignia of a Voroshilov[*] marksman. He's honestly earned the honor. The boys

[*] Kliment Voroshilov: Soviet general and defense minister, later president of the Soviet Union.

respect him and obey his orders. Now they feel guilty and sidle into the corners, along the walls. Grisha casts a glance at his "eagles." It's not hard for him to figure out what has gone on here. He feels like laughing when he sees Vladek, all wet and holding on to his shorts, and Avreml, soapy and hanging his head, dripping with water. But he mustn't laugh. If he's too easy on his "eagles," they'll tear each other to pieces. So he makes a serious face and scolds them. Then he sends Vladek to change his shorts, because soon there'll be an inspection and they need to prepare for morning roll call. Vladek has to leave, but not before he shakes a fist at Avreml, as if to say, "You wait, we'll meet again!" The boys accompany him smiling and wash themselves. Now they have to hurry. It's almost roll call. The bugle sounds again. They rush to put on their red neckerchiefs and run outside. The Pioneer troops assemble in four different groups arranged in circles, or "rings." One step in front of each circle stands its "ringleader," the Pioneer elected to be in charge. The ringleaders count their Pioneers to make sure that they're all present, and if someone's missing they find out why. Calling his circle to "Attention!" the ringleader reports to the captain of the troop (also a Pioneer elected by the troop). From the reports of the ringleaders, the captain puts together his roll call. Only then do they all assemble for inspection in the open space surrounding the flagpole, where the flag has remained lowered since last evening.

To the accompaniment of a resounding drumbeat, Valya leads the first troop to its appointed place, not far from the flag. She supervises the oldest children. The youngest are in the fourth troop. There the captain is a ten-year-old girl with a pair of short black pigtails that bounce around like the beard of a billy goat, which always makes Valya smile. A serious expression on her face, the girl marches to the beat of the drum, entirely absorbed by her assignment: every now and then she checks to see if her comrades are marching in line behind her. Finally, she brings them to their destination and breathes easier. Valya is proud of the little one. She's pleased to see how seriously this youngster takes her duties as captain. "Such a likable little cherub," she thinks, and feels the urge to pick her up in her arms. But she has to leave that for later. "You mustn't undermine the authority of a captain," Valya says to herself. "Some captain she would be if we carried her in our arms in front of her charges."

The whole camp has assembled in the meantime. All four drums strike three beats. "Attention!" Valya calls out and approaches Grisha, who's about eight meters away from her, in a red neckerchief. She salutes smartly. In a sharp, loud voice so all can hear, she announces: "Comrade Pioneer leader! The first troop numbers fifty-two. Fifty are present for the parade. Two are missing because of illness. All the others are well and ready to carry out today's plan. Captain Bielenkaya reporting. This is the end of the report." Again Valya raises her hand in the Pioneer salute. Grisha greets her in the same fashion and announces, "The report is accepted." Valya returns to her position. Looking around, she notices all the captains returning to their places, having given similar reports.

Now the Pioneer leaders take turns reporting to the senior Pioneer leader. She listens to carefully to get a good picture of what's happening in the camp. Everyone's eyes are turned toward her, Comrade Asya Grigorievna. She stands at attention before the flag, and it seems to Valya that her well-built body sits so firmly on her tanned slim legs, just like the statue of the female athlete in the park in Minsk. The statue is carved from white marble, so Valya doesn't know the color of the athlete's hair; but she thinks it must be dark blond. The eyes no doubt are blue-gray, and glittering on her tanned, energetic face. Otherwise, how could Asya and the statue be as alike as two peas in a pod? Valya must confess that she's noticed this strong resemblance only now, at the assembly. Why didn't it occur to her earlier? For she knows Asya Grigorievna from Minsk, where they were next-door neighbors. Her Pioneer leader was studying then at the Pedagogical Institute and was known simply as Asya. She liked to recite Pushkin, to sing the songs she had heard at the movies, and to play ball. Many of her student friends used to come to visit. Valya would politely make way for them if they met on the stairs. Later they stopped coming, because Asya had finished at the Institute and had gone away somewhere. Asya's mother told her that her daughter had been sent to work in the Western Territories.[*] When Valya's father and the whole family also moved to Bialystok for work, Valya once ran into Asya at the theater. She didn't meet her again until she came to the sanatorium. Here she finally saw her neighbor, now known as Asya Grigorievna, wearing a red neckerchief, looking just as she looks now near the flag. Valya is still gazing at her "statue." She's not surprised when she raises her hand in a salute. Asya Grigorievna announces today's program: after breakfast, fresh air in the woods, then play. Preparing for artistic self-expression. Dance, chorus, and recitation. After the late-morning snack: swimming and sunbathing by the Niemen. After lunch: a two-hour nap. After the afternoon snack: free play, meeting parents, artistic self-expression. After supper: one hour of free play, preparing for bed, evening roll call, then sleep.

All listen attentively. Today is an especially good day—Sunday! Everyone hopes that a family member will come: a mother, a father. Usually they bring regards from friends and acquaintances—also, fruit and sweets. Valya very much wants someone in her family to visit today. She wants them to see how beautifully she dances and how the sailor costume suits her. She looks so good in the long black trousers and the white sailor blouse. It's a pity that they don't take girls in the naval academies. Oh, how she'd sail on the ships, like a whirlwind! Not only that, but the middy blouse is tailor-made for her figure, and the cap with its ribbons sits so prettily on her head. . . .

The bugle sounds again. The drummers, too, are working at full blast. All stand at attention to the salute. The flag is raised up the pole. Slowly it rises, higher and higher, and with it the children's gaze. Finally it's secured at the top. The inspection is over. The day at camp begins.

---

[*] Territories annexed to the Soviet Union in 1939 and 1940, comprising Eastern Poland (including Bialystok), the Baltic states, Romanian Bessarabia, and Bukovina, as a result of the nonaggression pact signed by Stalin and Hitler.

Olik is lucky. All the boys are convinced of that. What else? All the older campers take turns on duty at the gate to the camp compound. But Olik's turn is today, of all days, and he'll be the first to know whose parents have come to visit. It's possible that over there, in that part of the woods, your mother could have been sitting for some time and you know nothing about it, since you'll be free to see her only after afternoon snack. But Olik stands at the gate, the first to see who's getting off the bus. He shares the other boys' sentiments and is very pleased with his post. Olik strolls about in front of the gate and every so often takes a peek at the red band on his left arm, which makes him feel so important. He imagines that the post he is guarding isn't really a children's sanatorium, but a vital strategic spot that's in serious danger. But from which direction? On the right lies the resort village of Druskenik, and on the left a pine forest. In front you can see the highway. Olik imagines that, over there, in the depths of the forest, an enemy is lurking. He must be vigilant. He strains his eyes and ears—trees, branches, and between them patches of sky. Quiet. Suddenly, there's a distant echo of horses' hooves. Olik listens. But this is no longer his fantasy, it is reality.

It's coming from the highway. Peasant wagons? He moves forward a few steps and takes in with a glance the spot where the road emerges from the forest. There's no one to be seen. But the pounding of the hooves comes closer. Now a thick cloud of dust rises up. From a distance, military wagons come into view, armed Red Army men, real artillery. "Maneuvers," he surmises at once, and his eyes light up brightly. "Real maneuvers." He'd love to see how things look in the field. He's already seen it in the movies, but that was just a few frames from the newsreel "News of the Day." Now he could sneak onto the field and he would see, with his very own eyes, how it all happens! But . . . he remains at his post. He knows very well that a Pioneer must under no circumstances desert his post, just like a soldier. What a shame. To miss out on such a moment!

These kinds of things don't happen every day. But one must not leave. Camp regulations forbid it. With a yearning glance he accompanies the detachment of Red Army men as it moves farther down the road until it is just a dot that vanishes in a thick cloud of dust. In his heart he's unhappy about the whole episode, but it's too late for regrets.

As he strides about, dissatisfied with himself, Olik notices a strange boy approaching. He seems to be about thirteen or fourteen years old. Whom does he want to see here? Olik decides to demonstrate the importance of his position, for the sake of which he renounced such a great pleasure. The strange boy wants to go through the gate. Olik blocks his way: "Whom do you want?" The boy apparently doesn't much care for the tone of voice in which Olik has spoken to him, and a frown appears on his forehead clearly signifying, "It's none of your business!" But he soon remembers why he came and decides that this is no time for confrontation. He tells Olik that it's urgent that he see Willy G; he has very important news to give him. Olik has little confidence in this young fellow. "I can imagine the kind of important news he's bringing. He'll have to wait." He explains rather coldly that, unfortunately, he can't let him in. Visiting hours today are from five to eight in the evening. Evidently the boy hadn't expected such an answer. He reflects a while. "How do I remove this unexpected obstacle? Should I tell him, or not?" He hesitates for a minute, but seeing that Olik is being stubborn, he realizes that he has no choice. Otherwise he won't be able to see Willy, any more than he can see his own ears. He takes Olik by the sleeve and whispers confidentially in his ear: "Did you see?" Olik doesn't appreciate this stranger's familiarity. He steps back a bit and asks coldly, "What?" The boy points with one finger in the direction of the highway. Olik is disappointed. You call that news? Of course I saw. Maneuvers. So what? Is that what he has to tell Willy so urgently? Well, he can wait. The stranger is disappointed that Olik isn't excited by the news. He thinks for a while about how to surprise him. He bends toward his ear and whispers, "War!"

Olik pulls back with a start. He gives him a sharp look. The boy makes a serious face, which at the same time expresses a certain triumph, as if to say, "Now you see what kind of urgent news!" Olik is somewhat upset by the news, but he doesn't want to believe it. What if he's lying? As if reading his thoughts in his eyes, the other boy speaks up again: "War with Germany! Molotov spoke on the radio.[*] On my honor as a Pioneer!" Now Olik no longer has any doubts. So these weren't maneuvers. It's a real war. There's a strange sensation in his heart. He doesn't know whether to cry or rejoice. "Wars nowadays!" he thinks. "It's not at all like they tell us in books. Take the Patriotic War of 1812.[†] That was a real war. Also the civil war[‡] in 1917, the war in Spain in 1936.[§] But last year we fought the Finns,[#] and nobody even had a sense of being at war. If it hadn't been for the radio, nobody would have known about it."

The boy is still waiting for Olik's answer. With Olik standing there lost in thought he could be waiting forever, so he heads for the gate by himself. But Olik wakes up from his reverie, stops him again, and rings the bell. The camp orderly comes out. In a few words Olik informs him of the situation. The orderly is very frightened. He turns to the boy with a couple of questions. How does he know? What are people saying in town? The boy has nothing to say except that everybody is talking about Molotov's speech. They say that the Germans have bombed Minsk, Bialystok, Grodno, Vilna, and other cities. Everyone is headed for home. He's also come to call for Willy; they come from the same small town, Sokólka. The orderly agrees to give Willy a note, because he's not in camp right now— they're all at the Niemen. The boy isn't satisfied with this kind of outcome to the affair. But he has no choice. He has to hurry back to his sanatorium for lunch. He pulls a pencil and small notebook

---

[*] The surprise German attack on the Soviet Union on Sunday, June 22, 1941, was announced over Soviet radio not by Stalin, as might have been expected, but by Foreign Minister Vyacheslav Molotov.

[†] Napoleon's invasion of Russia.

[‡] The fighting between the Bolsheviks and their opponents in the years following the October Revolution of 1917.

[§] The Spanish Civil War between the Republican Loyalists and Franco's Nationalists lasted from 1936 to 1939.

[#] The "Winter War" of 1939–1940 was fought between the Soviet Union and Finland over strategic border territory near Leningrad (now St. Petersburg.)

out of his back pocket, tears out a page and scribbles: "Willy! Germany has attacked us without a declaration of war. We have to think about what to do. Come to the train station tonight at 3 A.M. Volodya." He quickly hands over the piece of paper and runs away in the direction that he came from. Olik folds the piece of paper and gazes pensively until the boy vanishes from sight. "Oh," he thinks, "the things that go on in this world!" But he can't keep this news to himself, and he doesn't let the orderly get away. For that matter, the orderly doesn't want to go. What should they do? Both boys know that a very important matter is in their hands.

Children's home, Karakulino, 1942

Lena's Diary

Wednesday, the 8th of October [1941], 10:00 in the morning

The irony of fate! Did I ever dream that I would be so far from home, in a remote village in Udmurtia? That I would be the ward of a children's home, part of a collective of children who are strangers to me, all alone in a foreign land? In a foreign land, what a cruel sound! How much it means to a person. . . . Now, nearing the end of the seventeenth year of my life, with my body in full bloom and full of energy, love of life, and the joy of youth, the year is dirty, muddy, in sleepy Sarapul. My days pass in idleness, in unending sorrow and yearning for home. Is home really a cot in the communal dormitory, my satchel, notebooks, and books that lie orphaned, waiting for the school year to start? No! My home is there—on the other side of the front, in Bialystok! I recall my street, the old house, my mother! Mama, where are you now? My home? It's you. It's Sorele, Moyshele, Papa, my friends. Where are Sorele Davidovsky, Moshe, Leyke, Zavl, Moyshl, Siomke, Chaim, Hershl, Shloyme, Niomke? My home is my school, my teachers. My home is Bialystok.

And where am I? Leaning against the little table, I sit on my cot near the window. Outside it's a fine, chilly autumn day. A bright shower of sunshine falls on the balcony. The trees on the grounds of the children's home stand calm and majestic. The cool breeze causes their proud heads to bow in a morning greeting. A dazzling light bathes the treetops. Everything calls out to life, to activity. A carpet of yellow leaves is spread out on the earth—soft, cold, and beautiful. Golden autumn! A clear, transparent sky, the bright blue of space. High up, a bird flies. The forest echoes with the sound of rifle practice. And me? What am I doing on this beautiful autumn day? I'm not in school, because classes have been suspended for the upper grades and the students are working on the *kolkhoz* [Soviet collective farm].

I read and think, overcome with longing. What is autumn like in my hometown? Just like it is here? Is it sunny, cold, festive? The boots of a German soldier trample on the yellow falling leaves on the boulevard, marching over the smooth pavement of the streets. A black swastika flutters in the chilly brightness. There, in the narrow streets, my mother hides from a blond beast in a brown shirt. My girlfriend hides her pretty face as she crosses the street. And per-haps? Perhaps our house was burned down long ago and left in ruins. Perhaps my mother, father, little sister, and little brother lie in the damp, cold earth. Perhaps my girlfriend is ill. Who can tell me the secret of their fate? Perhaps my best friends have ended their lives in a dark prison? Who can comfort my aching heart, ease this sorrow? If I had wings, I would fly to you. Enough, I cannot go on . . .

Friday the 10th of October [1941], 3:00 in the afternoon

Today I saw a victim of the bloody, pitiless Second Imperialist World War.* It wasn't someone who fell in the wet earthen trenches, not one of those who rot in foxholes, not a hero at the front, whose name could be celebrated by historians and poets. No, this was a ten-year-old victim, Itsik Gruboretsov! A mischievous little fellow with rosy cheeks. He had come with his twelve-year-old brother, Tolek, to Druskenik for a vacation and ended up, along with us, far from his home—White Russia [Byelorussia, now Belarus]—and his parents, here in Sarapul. Now he's drawn his last breath. Last night he expired, after lying unconscious for twenty-four hours. He didn't even recognize his father, who had managed to come to see him. He orphaned his family, and all of us as well! Stunned, we all stood by his red coffin, looking for the last time at his childish, but jaundiced and cold little face. . . . Ten-year-old Itsik! May the tears that we shed become a sea, and may those responsible for this war drown in it. That would be revenge for your untimely death!

Saturday the 11th of October [1941], 3:00 in the afternoon

Bleary late autumn. A cold, stinging rain falls without letup, a damp, angry wind whips your face, the earth is covered with rusty leaves and sparse, yellow mud. You can't leave the house. Even when the bugle calls you to the dining hall, you don't go willingly. Afterward, back to the room. I'm reading Heine's works in Russian translation. The original can't be had! Our children's home will soon be moving to Karakulino, 60 kilometers from here. When will we finally begin to live a more or less normal, productive life?

---

* The Soviets called both world wars "imperialist" in Lenin's sense of the term, that is, as manifestations of the last stage of capitalism.

Tuesday the 14th of October [1941], 10:00 in the morning

Yesterday was our director's birthday. Our teacher B. P. and all the children in my group decided that I should present him with our birthday greeting. I would rather not have done it, but I couldn't refuse. I couldn't explain to the audience the reason for my anger—his attitude toward my close friend. I emphasized that, besides taking care of our nourishment, he was now responsible for our training and education. For that we would very grateful to him. I'm not sure how he took it. Genya and Dosya were surprised at the esteem I expressed. After all, they also knew how he behaved. But I explained to them that I still had a score to settle with him. It was my situation in the orphanage that forced me into this compromise.

Friday the 17th of October [1941], 7:00 in the evening

Leyke, * *Leyke; what have you come to!*

Today classes resumed in the upper grades and I went to school. This school is entirely different in character from my school at home. The accursed war has taken away my home, my parents, teachers, friends! It's landed me deep in the Soviet Union, in order to take away my ideals, my country, my goal in life. Fate has spared my life so that I could suffer, so that I could see everything that is sacred to me go to ruin. I'm becoming a shadow of myself!

Nothing but weltschmerz, Heine's weltschmerz. Soon I'll be seventeen years old but I am a shadow . . .

Monday the 20th of October [1941], 1:00 in the afternoon

I just came from school. I was called on in Algebra, and answered well. The teacher was pleased. The same in Russian

---

* Lena's Yiddish nickname, diminutive for *Leja* (pronounced "Leya"), the Polish spelling of *Leah*. She adopted the Russian equivalent, *Lena*, during her years in the Soviet Union described in the diary.

Literature. I don't lag behind the class; on the contrary, it seems to me that a lot of the time I surpass it. Learning comes easily to me despite the fact that I study everything in Russian, not in Yiddish as I used to. I master the terminology well. In general, things are not going too badly.

Soon we'll be going to Karakulino. I don't feel like moving to such a remote village, worse than Sarapul. Sixty kilometers from a railway line! To study in a new school after further interruption! But nothing can be done about it.

Friday the 24th of October [1941], 6:00 in the evening

The journey is over! Tuesday we left [Sarapul], and Wednesday morning we arrived in Karakulino,[*] a typical village on the banks of the Kama. A filthy dump with small houses, mostly wooden, one storey. Our building is located in the center of the village, two steps from the school, the marketplace, the dining hall, the headquarters of the Komsomol, and the post office. Nothing has been arranged for us yet. It's a former school building. For the third night we've been sleeping on mattresses on the floor. We don't go to school yet. We lie on the floor and read all day long. (I got books at the library!) Even now I'm lying on the ground near the kerosene lamp, which I struggled to obtain. (Here it's a rare commodity!) And I'm writing. We begin school on Monday! It seems that I'll take classes starting at two in the afternoon. I'd like to get settled one way or another, wash myself, be a human being! A bath and a decent bed—that's now the dream of every one of us! It looks like things will be better here than in Sarapul, because, first of all, this is a rural area, so we get better food, though a lot less than the norm. Butter, cheese, sour milk, *pakhta*, a drink somewhat like cream. We get meat every day! But there are no electric lights here, so we sit in the dark. Even a night-light is hard to get! There are no movies or theaters. The only things left to us are books. But you can't even get a good book here. In 1937 the library burned down,

---

[*] Sarapul and Karakulino are located about 200 miles east of Kazan.

and now all that's left are a few dozen books on agriculture, which don't interest me at all. I'm living on an island. My girlfriends these days are Tanya, Genya, and Asya. Lately Genya and I have become very close. She represents a particular type: a girl raised among the sons and daughters of the Jewish upper middle class, with an energetic, cocky personality. Intelligent, sensitive, arrogant, sometimes even egotistical . . . in total constrast to my taste, it would seem! Yet we often think and act as one. We're connected, to a certain extent, by our view of life. We both aspire to something higher: we want to get an education! Gritting our teeth, fists clenched, we are committed to study, and we are learning.

Tanya is altogether different. She is simpler, nicer in character than Genya, and more proletarian in the background in which she was raised and educated. She has more modest ideas: she works as a counselor, doesn't wish to study further, doesn't even read. She doesn't think about herself and her future.

Asya is a weak person: nervous, capricious, refined, but a loyal friend! In my view, she has a negative character, but her sisterly kindness is welcome. All in all, the four of us get along well. Wonderfully! Circumstances have united us and drawn close four people with different personalities, attitudes toward life and our environment . . . We share everything here, don't keep separate accounts of money, or clothes. We're better than we were back home—all because of our common misfortune—this accursed war! Our families and friends are all in Bialystok. We are alone here. Still, little by little, we forget the past. Forgetting is a law of human memory. Without forgetting there would be no remembering. We've got to make peace with our fate. It's hard to imagine, hard to say out loud, but it seems to me that I'll never again see my home and my family. I'll have to build my life where I live now. It's hard to predict yet where fate will cast me, where I'll have to take root. But I doubt it could be the soil from which I sprung. I don't want to think about what will be. About what once was. It makes me too sad! I want to get on with my studies! That's the only way out. Though I'm no longer Leyke from Bialystok—only Lena from the Russian children's home, disappointed and grown old while still in my youth.

Monday the 27th of October [1941], 11:00 in the morning

Today we start going to school. Classes begin at two o'clock in the afternoon. But my mood is not good: there's depressing news from the front. The Germans have captured Stalino,*part of the Donbas. Bitter fighting is taking place in the region near Kharkov. Our fate is sealed. I'm not expecting a miracle.

Yesterday Genya and I went to the outskirts of the village. We talked about our fate, our life. We came to the conclusion that we've both fallen very low. We're forced to think about practical things; we've become greedy like everyone around us, because we don't get enough to eat. Still, we're better off than the rest. Since we have a little money left, we can still afford to buy some things. But the food sticks in our throats when people look at us greedily; we share with the others at the children's home. Yet, we are judged guilty because of our beggarly mouths.

I have problems with the director as well—he goes to great lengths to humiliate and insult me, because I don't flatter him . . . because I speak Yiddish with my roommates. Yesterday he spoke condescendingly about Jewish schools. It hurt me a lot. Then he wanted to show that I don't know Polish: he argued for three hours about whether it's correct to say *uczyc sie na inzyniera* [to study to be an engineer]. He didn't succeed in proving that it's wrong. He's terribly irritating. I want to be rid of the children's home, of the director. But how can I help myself? Even if I gave up my studies and found some sort of work, I still couldn't live on my own. My loneliness gives me great pain and suffering. Life is base and hateful!

Yet I study with dedication, do my homework conscientiously, as is my habit.

---

* Today Donetsk, a major city in the Donbas, or the Donets Basin, an important industrial region in eastern Ukraine.

Tuesday the 28th of October [1941], 10:00 in the morning

Yesterday I went to school. What a low level! A real village school. I can see that this school will give me nothing. The teachers explain the material poorly. The class knows nothing. There's still a chance to enroll in a children's home in Sarapul, where I could study. The teachers there are very good. But I don't want to go. The news from the front is alarming. Who knows what tomorrow may bring. I don't want to cut myself off from the collective and fall into an even greater isolation. Incidentally, the food there is even worse, much worse. Here (where we starve gradually) it's a paradise, comparatively speaking. Let things go on as they are.

Wednesday the 29th of October [1941], 10:30 in the morning

I want to curse, to pour out my bitter heart somewhere! Soon I won't be able to take it anymore! How long will I lie around on the ground in a room with thirty-five loudmouthed girls? How long will I be humiliated by the director? The fact that it's obvious that I don't want to flatter him, that I don't care about his opinion of me, that his silly jokes don't interest me, makes him hostile.

I suffer from hunger here, I always want to eat, even when I leave the table, so sometimes I think: what difference does it make? The hell with it, I'll leave this wretched institution, the village school and I'll go to work in a big city like Izhevsk. Then I realize that I'd be even more isolated there, have even less to eat. Because even for money you can't get more than 400 grams of bread a day. You can forget about butter, cheese, a tiny bit of meat, even some porridge. If I had been starving at home, it would have been easier for me! Here my suffering is physical and mental! Here for breakfast I get a serving of scolding and veiled sarcasm. Here I feel like a bird in a cage. When will this cursed war end?

Thursday the 30th of October [1941], 9:00 in the morning

Moments of quiet pain. Deep in my heart sits a little worm that eats and eats away. I long for peace, for home. I had a strange dream last night: I'm sitting in the house, where there's a boat with live fish—sunfish and carp. My mother sits in the boat, also Sorele and Moyshele; we're supposed to sail away somewhere. They're waiting for me! Here the thread of my dream breaks off; I wake up on the filthy mattress in the cold room. Why am I not crying? Slowly my soul begins to quiver. Mama, hear how my heart cries out! Look at how pale my face is and how sad the look in my eyes. Remember me kindly! I don't want to disappear so soon into the eternity of oblivion. Sorele Davidovsky, do you still remember me? Does my image sometimes appear before your beautiful dark eyes? If I could, I would send you flowers, little blue ones. A modest request—forget me not!

The same day, 6:00 in the evening

I'm writing in school during a break. I've just learned that on the twenty-fourth of this month the government was transferred from Moscow to Kuybyshev.[*] Only the Defense Committee and Stalin remained in Moscow. This morning the radio announced that the Germans had taken Kharkov and that Moscow was heavily bombed last night. I'm worried about what will happen.

The same day, 9:00 in the evening

Once again I'm in an agitated state. The reason is quite simple: yesterday there was a general assembly while I was in school. When I returned, they told me that I'd been unanimously elected to the children's council, and to great applause! Today there

---

[*] Soviet name for Samara, a city on the middle Volga some 530 miles southeast of Moscow, to which most of the government was evacuated as the German forces approached the capital.

was a meeting of the council. Everyone was prepared to elect me as chair. I knew in advance that the director wouldn't be very pleased. He reacted sharply to my proposals for the program, which were supported by the majority of the members! It was a personal attack! I see that we'll never be compatible. He came into the room to see how the lessons were going. We got involved in a discussion about Russian and Yiddish. We finally got into the subject of whether to study and speak Yiddish or not. I eagerly joined the discussion, maintaining that it's fine to speak Yiddish! I gave him lots of arguments, proving that it hasn't prevented us from learning Russian. He couldn't prove the contrary. So he said good night and left. The young people—formerly students at Yiddish schools—were happy and laughed. It gave me great pleasure. All his dried-up phrases . . . ha, ha, ha.

Saturday the 1st of November [1941], 9:00 in the morning

The news about the political situation makes the blood freeze in my veins. Today the Soviet radio announced clashes on the eastern frontier. In other words, Japan also will seize some territory. We are lost. The situation now is worse than in 1918. At that time the revolutionary position was strong. Now, unfortunately, the army is weak. The anniversary of the Revolution is rapidly approaching. What present will the nation bring to its birthday? Volodya, who was in the military hospital in Sarapul, says that the wounded soldiers are happy that they're no longer at the front.

Scabies has erupted among us at the children's home. The epidemic devours almost everyone. It's no wonder: you can't wash yourself, you sleep on the ground on a filthy mattress, and on top of that—two to a mattress! The overwhelming majority are sick. I am still healthy. What will happen later, I don't know. I'm doing well in my studies, I get excellent reports. But I'm not satisfied.

Monday the 3rd of November [1941], 8:30 in the morning

Yesterday there was a general assembly, and I was elected chair of the children's council to loud applause. Why do the children like me so much? After all, most of them don't know Leyke from Bialystok. They don't know about my underground Pioneer work,[*] about my social activities in school. What do they see in me?

The institution is in general in a state of disorder. We still sleep on the ground, although some boards are lying around in the courtyard. The older boys sawed a few boards, but when the girls wanted to wash them for the beds, there was no water available. Even water to drink is also unavailable. Why doesn't everyone think about providing water from the well? After all, we have to wash, too. The entire institution has lice! The director demands a lot from everyone, except from himself. Yesterday he yelled at the cleaning woman, who came with us from Druskenik: "You do nothing! I'll drive you out like a dog!" How can you talk that way to a woman?

Yesterday three children from the home sold a shirt and a sweater at the market for eleven rubles. One of the teachers, Fanny P., noticed and spoke to the director. They're all demanding that I come out publicly against them, that I denounce the children at an assembly! I understand that we must fight against such phenomena, but I take pity on the children. I understand that they were driven to it by hunger. How often am I hungry myself? A good manager could avoid second-rate food products and provide bread. Especially since we're in the country, with collective farms all around.

I explain to the children that clothes are very necessary, that without them we'll catch cold. So — don't sell anything! I also tell the director that we need to install a faucet on the premises so that we'll have water to drink and wash ourselves!

---

[*] In pre-1939 Poland, the Pioneer youth movement was illegal.

Tuesday the 4th of November [1941], 9:00 in the morning

Yesterday, before going to school, Genya and I both spoke with the headmistress, Rebecca Izraelevna, about life in the children's home. Rebecca Izraelevna thinks that our work could and should go better than it has up to now, despite the difficult circumstances. She gives us the example of her life in 1924, when there was a terrible famine. People were dropping in the streets from hunger and epidemics, and still she brought up her son to be an honest, productive person. Why can't we bring up such decent people here? Because here there are no educators who truly love the children and feel close to them. Lately, even the director—she characterized him very accurately!—doesn't concern himself much with the children. And, furthermore, he is no educator! He's a capable person, lacking in native intelligence, but with practical experience. He doesn't try to improve himself. His decisions are inconsistent. Recently he's neglected his work altogether, because he's busy taking care of his sister and getting her settled among us. He's provided her with a room and a bed, and a blanket to make into a coat! But the children are hungry and suffering from the cold . . .

Today in class we're supposed to write a composition on Russian literature. It will be interesting to see how I'll write it.

Wednesday the 5th of November [1941], 12:30 in the afternoon

All the upper grades went to the Kama River today to saw wood that belongs to our school. I also went and worked for an hour and a half. Then I got tired, my feet were cold, and I went back to the home. I admire my schoolmates—boys and girls, peasant children, healthy, used to hard physical labor. They'll always be able to manage. As for me, they say that I wasn't too bad with a saw. But I tire quickly. I'm not used to it.

I had another confrontation with the director today. When I got up in the morning to work at the Kama, he sent word for me not to put on my coat because I'd tear it, and he would not allow that. (Meanwhile, he hasn't paid me for the coat yet!) That's good, I thought. It would truly be a waste of a good coat, and where would I find another? I put on my pants and a dress and a jacket. When he took a look at me, he said he wouldn't allow me to walk around without a coat, because I'd catch cold. That's good too, I thought. He's concerned about my health.

"I'll wear my coat as far as the river," I explained. I'll take it off there, because it gets very warm sawing wood. Then he began to insist that I not go to work, that I ask the school principal to be excused. At first I didn't understand his motives. That he, a Party member, should give such advice . . . Then I understood: his cousin's daughter, Shura—I'll write about her separately—didn't want to go, therefore he didn't want me to go. That way he doesn't lose face with the students, teachers, and school administration. A rotten piece of advice!

Thursday the 6th of November [1941], 5:30 in the evening (during an algebra lesson)

Yesterday I received a Good+ for my work in Russian class. I made three mistakes in idiomatic expressions, but not a single grammatical, spelling, or stylistic mistake! This means that I've made a certain amount of progress in mastering the Russian language!

Today I got a 5 [the highest grade] for my class work in algebra. I'm considered an Honors student and was called to have my picture taken, so that my photograph could hang among the Honors students. I didn't go.

My entire time here I haven't had a bath. I loathe myself—I'll probably rot from the filth. A little hot water! We suffer from the cold: it's been more than two weeks since they heated up a stove. At night it's very cold, by day it's even worse. Our bread ration is always being reduced. We all joke about how we're shrinking.

Lately I often think about home. I dream that I'm in the house and talking with Mama, with my friends. I spare my mother all the work. I do it all for her. I'm even ready to sacrifice my studies to help her materially. I dream of a bourgeois, peaceful life—Mama, and Papa, too, provided with food, clothing, and housing. While Sorele goes to school and studies, Moyshl works, and I work and study. I'm surrounded by warm parental love and I embrace the family with loving care. Around me are my friends—boys and girls. We study together, have fun, discuss life's problems. It's all peaceful and good!

Unfortunately, this paradise exists only in my dream. I myself am in hell. Kazan[*] has been bombed again. They are fighting at the gates of Moscow. We've heard no other news. For more than a week, there's been no new information. I'm worried about Khone's situation. He went away a month ago and hasn't come back yet. What can it mean? Maybe Tambov,[†] too, has become a war zone and he can't get out?

Saturday the 8th of November [1941], 8:00 in the morning

The day before yesterday, that is, on the evening of the sixth, there was a program devoted to the twenty-fourth anniversary of the October Revolution. A group from the children's home also performed. The mood was comparatively solemn. After the ceremony we went off to the club. It had some electric lighting (a weak generator was operating), which in itself added to the solemnity. The director bought ice cream for everybody. The assembled intelligentsia enjoyed the performance by our children.

Yesterday we attended a meeting. In the middle of the square stood a platform hung with flags. Koleshnikov, director of the *Raisoviet* [district council], spoke. One thing struck me: except for us and the middle-school students, the only ones present were a few people who live near the marketplace—no representatives from the collective farms or organizations. Following a half hour of speeches, we went home. There was a ceremonial lunch at the

---

[*] Major city on the Volga near its confluence with the Kama, some 200 miles from Sarapul.

[†] City 300 miles southeast of Moscow, well away from the front.

children's home, attended by some of our teachers and representatives of Soviet—and Party—organizations. There were some speeches. The mood was truly solemn.

After lunch we had a group dance performance and an amateur talent show. I have just one question: what was responsible for the atmosphere? Was it the presence of guests? Or the splendid, almost princely, lunch? Chicken, soup with rice, stewed fruit. . . . For supper—milk and cookies! Our group had not eaten as well in a long time! I heard people talk among themselves, "More holidays like this!" Why not, I thought.

Today, a day after the celebration, bread was again in short supply at breakfast. So, once more I'm hungry. It turns out that holiday cookies can't fill you up for the whole year. It's amazing how much I have changed! My stomach is no idealist. It doesn't want to know how dangerously close to death the country has come.

The same day, 10:30 at night

Today a group of evacuees arrived from Moscow and Yaroslav—a thousand people. For seventeen days they dragged themselves—by train, steamer, in small boats. Many of them fell ill along the way. Mostly Jews have arrived. Now you hear a lot of Yiddish! Looking at this newest batch of homeless, the rows of packages, the wandering through Karakulino snowstorms—it tears at my heart.

Now I see that we are more fortunate. We already have a place to rest our heads, we already have a bed. We don't get much to eat, but still we're not starving. And then there's the opportunity to study, which has always been, and still is today—today more than ever—the most important thing in my life! This has remained with me from the past: my little bit of knowledge and a burning thirst for more knowledge and skill. Unfortunately, I cannot get much in Karakulino, where the school is inferior and the library poor. Still, I read rigorously and try to obtain supplementary materials for the subjects I've passed. I'm very popular with the students and the teachers at school. There are some pretty good kids in the class. Ordinary peasant sons and daughters, not very intelligent, a simple bunch with low intellectual standards, but very good companions. I want to get to know something about their private lives. I'm thinking of visiting somebody at home. Until now I haven't had the time. How strange my situation is now. I am becoming more mature. I feel the young, hot, blood flowing. I long for tenderness, but nobody close to me is here. Volodya Leonov, a sixteen-year-old Russian boy, well-built, tall, handsome, is not indifferent to me, but we have nothing in common. He's childish in his way of thinking, hasn't experienced what I have. He can't understand me. It's up to me to take care of myself, to help myself.

Tuesday the 11th of November [1941], 11:30 (during a free period in school)

Today is a beautiful, frosty day, -18° C. Deep snow, bright sunshine. I don't feel cold. My coat, made from a Lithuanian cotton quilt, is very warm. It warms me by day and by night. I put it on top of my blanket. I'm wearing flannel underpants. The winter here is very beautiful—a blinding whiteness all around and a blueness of sky. I'm becoming cheerful.

When I see Volodya I also feel a warmth coursing through me. I know that he ought to be different: he should hold high spiritual ideals, and be clever, serious, intelligent. But, unfortunately, handsome, physically well-developed, but childishly good-natured Volodya doesn't have these qualities. Yesterday, as I sat reading in Asya's room, which is separated from his room by a thin partition, he kept yelling out, "Lena!" He spoke to me and sang me love songs. I didn't answer. He tell jokes, hangs around. But nothing will come of it!

Yesterday a closed Komsomol [Young Communist League] assembly was held at the children's home. I was elected deputy secretary. Asya declined a position as senior Pioneer leader. When she was compelled to accept she became upset and later even cried.

She told me about the bad mood she has been in lately. I understand her very well. She now works as a seventh grade teacher. But she can't help them when they do their homework; she's always asking me how to explain things to them. She has lost her authority with the children. She finds the work very hard. Now she misses her "mother," that is, the woman who adopted her, since she never knew her parents. An unhappy girl! She also spent her youngest years in a children's home. Then this woman, an engineer, adopted her. She never enjoyed a real mother's love, she has nobody in this world. In 1940 she went to work. Now she is here. But the work does not satisfy her. Things are going badly, and she can't make them better. I feel sorry for her. She's not too intelligent, badly educated, has no real interests in life besides her material needs.

Wednesday the 12th of November [1941], 2:00 in the afternoon

The material situation has improved a bit. You can now get a little more bread. Lately I'm less hungry. The teachers in school have treated us well. They worry because we have no felt boots—the temperature is -22° [C]—and no gloves. Maybe we'll get them soon? Olga Petrovna, the seventh grade classroom teacher, who teaches geography, is especially nice. Everyone feels sympathy for us. But, on the whole, we actually have better living conditions than the local population—after all it's a children's home! The only problem is that there's no place to do your homework. The seventh graders make a lot of noise, and in the room where we sleep together I can't study. I have to go away to the younger children.

Thursday the 13th of November [1941], 2:00 in the afternoon

Yesterday was a very good day for me! I accomplished a great deal—prepared a classroom composition in Russian Literature, and I washed myself!! (I was barely able to wheedle a little hot water from the kitchen.) I also read two hundred pages of my book, *Oblomov* by Goncharov.

After I had a wash I cheered up! I got into bed, waited until the girls finished their homework, then took the lamp, placed it on a chair near my bed, and read for a long time, until late in the day. It was very interesting. I finished the book. Now I'll do it all the time. I have to read a lot, develop myself.

Friday the 14th of November [1941], 4:00 in the afternoon

Here there are always big freezes, though they call them little ones: -24°, -25° C. In our institution it's very cold: they provide no heat, since there's no wood. We are freezing. The youngsters get into bed to do their homework.

Today I dreamed about my mother! She sits alone in the house. Nobody is there with her. It breaks my heart. It's so peculiar. I pity her! I'm so homesick for her. For sixteen years she fed me, allowed me to study. I remember how many sleepless nights she spent at my bedside when I had the measles, or was ill with scarlet fever, or with an inflammation of the lungs. When I lay in the hospital in a hopeless condition she would visit me twice a day. When I fell ill she was always with me. And when I was well, she prepared everything, cleaned up, took care of everything. Who loved me as she did? Who else rejoiced in my achievements ? Day in, day out, every hour and minute, she worked to take care of the family. How much beauty there is in a mother's nature, in the instinct born in a woman. Who can repay her for the care she showed us, for the hardship we gave her? Mama, forgive me for all the trouble I caused you and for which I never was able to repay you! A gruesome hand has painfully cut me off from your healthy tree trunk. A mighty storm has tossed me far away and compelled me to flourish. . . . Mama, I love you! Where are you? Where are you living? Who's taking care of you now? Who consoles you in your hard times?

Monday the 17th of November [1941], 7:00 in the evening

Yesterday was a Sunday. We cleaned up our rooms, washed the windows, tables, chairs, and floors. Then we washed ourselves in the bath. I was very pleased yesterday, despite having to bring our own water from the well to heat and then in the bathhouse—a narrow, dark ruin—having the terrible thick smoke sting our eyes. The door was open the whole time and we shivered from the cold, yet we bathed totally naked. After all, it's a pleasure to wash and be clean. Yesterday I discovered my body. I don't know why now in particular. Maybe I haven't looked at myself in a long time. Maybe it's in itself a sign of maturity. In any case, I found my body attractive. Really — a healthy, young, pink, hot girl's body, a slender, graceful figure, an object that can confer pleasure, and strives to do so. Although — there is still time! Meanwhile, there's no one who attracts me. Not even Volodya.

Friday the 21st of November [1941], 11:00 in the evening

Our headmistress, Rebecca Izraelevna, is a very intelligent, clever woman. She is the sort of person who earns respect through her understanding. An older woman, a splendid organizer, a good educator, she truly could be the head of an institution. But here she cannot do it. She doesn't get along with our director: if she says "one," he says "two." Naturally, he prevails. The teachers don't like her because she demands a lot from them for the sake of the children. Some of the children don't understand her, and sometimes judge her badly, because she criticizes them, and that—as everyone knows—is not a pleasant thing. In return, the older, more perceptive children are on her side; they understand and appreciate her! On the whole, she is energetic and likable. People like that are usually not appreciated, because they don't show themselves off in all their glory, don't sing their own praises—like our director—but do their work day in, day out, honestly and well, without asking for thanks or praise. The work itself is their satisfaction. Unfortunately, there are few such people. And they are ruled over by chatterboxes who actually know nothing. For example, our director, who doesn't know the first thing about teaching or how to oversee our education.

We are having an epidemic of scabies. No end of mangy children, almost half the group. This includes even many of the older, always clean children, girls. There's no salve to heal them. They all lie together—dirty, isolated—in a big ward. They found scabs and lice among many of the younger ones. There's nothing that can heal them, either. Everyone is so depressed. Those who are still healthy are jittery: Maybe I've caught it too? When will the epidemic start eating away at me? I'm very afraid. Health conditions here are not the best, so maybe I, too, will get sick? Every morning I examine my body, especially the hands, between the fingers. For now it's clean, I'm healthy. But who knows what will happen later. Tanya had scabies in Sarapul, it was never cured, and now there are suppurating ulcers on her hands. She lies in bed, but she has no medication.

Today the radio announced that Kerch[*] has been evacuated. Every time another city is taken. What will be the end? Will the Nazis really destroy cities and people, stamp out ancient cultures? Could it be that we'll have to stay here until the last soldier and the last red flag have fallen? What a sad fate! What do we see in our life? Calamities near and far, pain, destruction, filth.

Sunday the 23rd of November [1941], 12:00 noon

Last night I went to a private peasant bathhouse. It's a small room in a stable, well heated. I washed myself well. Now I'm standing at the stove in the dormitory, reading a book. The room is clean, quiet, calm. Everybody is reading or writing. It feels cozy and homelike. But when you stop to think that, at this very moment, soldiers are falling at the front, there are women in trenches, then your soul is on fire! How will this bloody drama come to an end?

---

[*] Strategically located city in the eastern Crimea.

Yesterday, in the boys' wing, 200 rubles were stolen from the cleaning woman. Rebecca Izraelevna wanted to notify the police, or to send someone to the marketplace to see who might be buying something. But I advised her that it would be better to do a search! She did it first thing in the morning, and Mindlin was caught. His father is a Hero of the Soviet Union.

Now a trial by his comrades will certainly begin. By Rebecca Izraelevna's actions you can see that she's an energetic woman. The director is in Izhevsk.* If he were here, he would yell, threaten, and nothing would come of it—as usual.

Wednesday the 26th of November [1941], 12:00 noon (during a physics class)

The last two days I've been feeling very sad. I miss my home more than ever. In class I'm not very attentive. That doesn't prevent me from answering the questions that are put to me and even from getting good reports. What will be in the future? When will the war end? When will I finally be able to go home? When will I be able to see my parents, my family, my friends? I write their first and family names on the cover of my notebook. Life is gray, dark, as the days are now. I yearn for the excitement of the big city, for our culture, for a good book, a good play, movie, or concert, for our community, for our interesting life! Who has the right to deny me my wishes? The teacher asked me just a few minutes ago for my pen, but I didn't hear him. I was too busy scribbling. Then I realized what was going on, and it was unpleasant. The whole class was staring at me.

* The nearest big town.

Thursday the 27th of November [1941], 11:00 in the morning

We were supposed to have a history class now, but the teacher, Mikhail Ivanovich, has been summoned to the *Voyenkomat* [military draft board]. At two o'clock he'll be leaving to join his division. It seems that the physics teacher, Nikolai Fedorovich, will also be mobilized. The school will be left without teachers. Who knows when they'll get some new teachers, especially women, to replace them. The situation is becoming more serious. A Red Army group has just arrived on furlough. We looked at them, all worn out, through the windows of our classroom. Here they can forget about the war; only the poor conditions and the mobilization are reminders. This, after all, is deep in the country's hinterland.

One thing puzzles me: Mikhail Ivanovich is, after all, an invalid: during the Finnish War he lost the thumb on his right hand. Why have they called him up now? He cannot use weapons. But he can serve as a *Politruk;*[*] he's intelligent and an active Komsomol member.

Friday the 28th of November [1941], 11:00 in the morning (during a class on Darwinism)

It's half a year already that I'm away from home—half a year in which I haven't seen a Yiddish book, newspaper, or journal. I long for Yiddish literature, to see Yiddish in print. It seems to me that I've already forgotten the literary language. At times I have to struggle to translate an easily understood Russian word into Yiddish. How annoying that is! The thought that I may have to spend long years in this environment, that I'll forget Yiddish more and more, makes me very sad.

---

[*] Political instructor attached to a Soviet military unit.

Saturday the 29th of November [1941], 11:00 in the morning (during a trigonometry class)

"He" returned from his trip very upset. He got quite a dressing-down for his work. In the *Narkompros* [Department of Education], they were already considering whether to remove him from his position. But Asya, who accompanied him, strongly defended him. She's been chasing him all along. Straightaway he started scolding the older children, had bad things to say about the Jewish children, just like a real anti-Semite. But he tries to convince me that he has Jewish blood in his veins, that he considers himself a Jew! He is an ugly type, that's what he is!

The first quarter has come to an end. I'm a full-fledged Honors student! But for me it's only a small satisfaction. There will be no vacation this year.

The same day, 8:00 in the evening

Tomorrow is my birthday—seventeen years old on the thirtieth of November! The most beautiful years of a person's life. For me, they are lost; joy is forbidden. Last year at this time, Sorele bought me a present, and then I bought one for her. Last year I was home, in my environment, at ease with myself. And now? In a children's home where I'm totally dependent on the mood and whims of the director, of educators . . . an object of educational experiments, a theme for gossip on the part of officials, who can label a person: "Eats too much, eats too little, is obedient or not, proud or obstinate, or has a slavish nature." Last year I was an independent person, appreciated in society, a thinking person. Today I am a zero.

Enough about myself! Mama! Is she alive? Who in my family is alive? And if they are alive, do they still remember the date of my birthday? Mama, don't cry over the death of your daughter! Do not cry, because she is alive and well, and also because she's not worth your noble tears. While I was at home, I helped you very little, I was busy with my studies, my girlfriends and boyfriends, community activities. Mama, forgive me! At home no one understood you, not Papa, not Moyshl, not Sorele—they were too young. I was the only one who knew your past, the time of your childhood: when you wanted to get an education and your mother didn't approve. I sensed your loneliness when your mother died. I learned of your suffering during the thirteen years that you served your older sister. Mama, what kind of happiness did you ever have in your life? You had hopes for your children. What did they bring you? I, who understood you and sympathized with you, how did I help you? If only I still could! Let's meet again so that I can bring you warm greetings and loving thanks. For you are a wonderful angel! What a pity that until I was sixteen I did everything only for myself, and little to help you. Mama, don't shed any tears on my birthday! The tears stick in my throat. If I were younger and nearby, perhaps they would wash away my guilt. Now it's too late and impossible. I'm sure that you mourn for me and suffer. But I'm alive, I'm healthy, I'm getting an education. My fate has saved me!

I remember the story about the mother who lost her beautiful hair and eyesight looking for the soul of her child. Remember, you told it to me once. You lost your health, your youth, to your children. Mama, only someone who has lost you can appreciate your worth! Now I remember how we read stories together. Do you remember—*The Little Boy With the Ring, The Ugly Duckling, The Daisy*? Remember how we used to cry reading *Shlumperl* or *The Story About the Wicked Stepmother and the Poor Shoemaker*? In my memory there lives your *Old Rope-Spinner, The Shepherd With the Flute*. Remember how comical they were when they danced, the rolling pin stuck to the sheep, the innkeeper's wife to the rolling pin, the umbrella to the innkeeper's wife, the priest to the umbrella! Oh . . . then, when I heard the story from your enchanting mouth, or read it along with you, I really was your "clever little Leyele," who dreamed of making her mother happy, making her into a real lady, dressing her in gold and satin, bringing good fortune to Shlumperl, to the poor little bird, to the modest daisy— to all those who suffer, who are humiliated and rejected! Then I was a naïve little dreamer with little understanding and a lot of emotion—but now. . . . What good is my knowledge—I have no heart!

When I was little, we lived together, sharing our feelings. When I got older—wiser, in the opinion of the world—we parted, because you remained a simple woman of the people, the mother who loved me, and I became a *gymnazistke.*[*] Unfortunately for me, my feelings disappeared. Remember when at age five I went to stay with Grandma, how I missed you! After two weeks I came back and jumped into your lap, nestled my head in your breast and wept like a silly child.

Until the fifth grade I used to tell you everything, share all my experiences, and you listened to me so wisely, understanding everything. You never told me that I was a silly little thing, that I'm talking foolishness. You would stroke my head and pretend that I was telling you serious things. In 1934 we lived in particularly difficult circumstances, remember? I had no shoes in the winter and I had foot problems. You convinced me to wear Yudl's big-boy shoes, but I didn't want to, and cried. I was ashamed to wear somebody's hand-me-down shoes, that's why I wailed. You stroked my head and told me how you suffered as an orphan when you were a child, when everyone insulted you, no one cared about you, and you wore rags. I saw the tears in your eyes, and so I put on the hated shoes and went to school. The same year we suffered terrible hardship. I saw how you wept silently, how you hoarded every morsel of bread for us—the children. When Papa came with a loaf of bread, we all rejoiced, because that same day at the marketplace they had stolen your last two zlotys.

In 1936 I was very ill. You didn't leave my bedside, you sold all the household goods, skimped on everyone's food, most of all your own, and took me to doctors at the hospital. Then you arranged nursing care and restored my feeble health.

I remember how you felt for me when I cried the time Papa forced his way into the theater where I was performing. Now I understand that he was right: he wanted to see his daughter per-

[*] Yiddish: female student in a *gymnazium,* roughly high school, but rather more prestigious.

form, see with his own eyes what it was that everyone praised. But he couldn't even afford the 50 *groshn* [Yiddish: half a zloty] for the upper balcony. That's why there was a scandal behind the curtain and I was so ashamed. I cried, and screamed at Papa. But, you understood and sympathized.

In seventh grade I was already earning money. That's the root of the tragedy. At first—the joy we both felt. Remember, how happy you were when with my money you bought fabric to make me a dress: pink flowers on a black background, gathered in front with a red band. We were both proud and happy.

Later—the *gymnazium*. I studied and tutored younger children and I earned money. In so doing I set myself apart from your fate and from my brother and sister. I started to dress better (with my own money). Sorele and Moyshele quietly envied me and gradually they began to respect me. I became privileged in the house. Remember the incident with Papa about my coat? All summer I saved money for a coat (I was giving five lessons a day), because the old coat that Henye had given me was worn out. I asked Ettl to sew the coat for me. Papa was jealous then, because his old fur coat was ragged and shabby. He needed a new coat, too. But he had no money. From your perspective, Mama, I was the one who had to be better dressed, because I went among gymnazium students and I worked until late at night. . . . Mama, do you remember the short story I wrote for the *Olympiad* [a writing competition at the school]— "Mirl"? There I described the nature of my work at the time and your attitude toward it. Unfortunately, I don't have it with me now, but you'll find it at home. It's a shame that I didn't make the time then to think about your situation. I truly was working a lot—studying and teaching others, hardly sleeping or eating, involved in my everyday cares and not thinking about you. Your inquisitiveness frightened me, so I kept quiet. I talked with my friends more than with you.

Now I feel guilty and my mistake pains me! How can I correct it? What can I do for my mother? I can't even wipe away a tear from her eyes, can't send her a single word of consolation. Maybe she's suffering hardship? Fate, take me back to my mother! I must help her, make sacrifices for her.

Sorele Davidovsky! Perhaps the date the thirtieth of November reminds you of something. Maybe you'll give some thought to your old friend. You're probably thinking that I did not live to see my seventeenth birthday, that my body is already cold and dead. You're wrong, my dear. I am a worse cripple: a cold breath in a warm body, an extinguished faith, a sullied ideal, a disillusioned shadow . . . because I'm no longer the same Leyke that you loved. I am a dull creature who cannot even weep over my fate. My dear, do you still remember our plans, my theory of ideal friendship, our "triple alliance" (you, me, and Zavl), the two camps (ours, and Yankl and Siomke's), our amusements? Remember how we used to reveal our feelings? Where are you now? How is it to live in an occupied land? Is our school still there, our teachers, our friends? Who is your best girlfriend or boyfriend? Don't forget me! Remember me as I was when we studied, read, thought, and dreamed together.

Where are you now, my friends, all the boys and girls? Perhaps in the dark dungeon of a German prison? Perhaps in the forest with the Red partisans? Perhaps you are depressed under the reactionary Nazis, disillusioned, desperate? It may be that your fate is much worse than mine. Things are bad for all of us. I'd like to say a few words of consolation to you, but forgive me, it's not possible. Perhaps we'll meet yet again, see each other in better times.

Sunday the 30th of November [1941], 3:00 in the afternoon

What a peculiar day! First thing in the morning Fanny P., one of our teachers, wished me happy birthday and gave me a kiss! I was deeply touched—a woman I hardly know showing such cordiality and maternal affection. All this at a time when I feel lonely, forgotten, and abandoned. Afterward we went off to a Sunday volunteer project and until noon we cleaned out a big, dirty stable. When I returned, Rebecca Izraelevna greeted me warmly, saying that her wish for me was that I might see my parents again soon. She gave me a kiss and a present, a book by Levitan,* which is hard to find in this village. That touched me even more. I ran into the room, threw myself on the bed, and burst into tears. Afterward I wrote a letter to Rebecca Izraelevna, thanking her warmly and expressing my feelings.

Right after that, Shura Zlatina—Fanny P.'s daughter and a classmate of mine—wished me a happy birthday and gave me Gorky's short stories. The inscription is very apt: "You cannot know the taste of sweetness until you have tasted bitterness."† A meaningful inscription, to the point, and all in Russian.

This evening we celebrated the end of the first quarter in the children's home and in school. Our group achieved brilliant results, received many awards and good grades. The group got two achievement banners in school. The Honors students were given prizes by the administration of the home. I received Lermontov's poetry. For each person the director wrote a special aphorism. For me he wrote Shosta Rustaveli's‡ "*Postoronniego Sovieta v Goriestyakh Poliezen Nam!* [In times of trouble, the advice of others is useful to us."] and an inscription: "*Lena, vyed tvoya tvorcheskaya zhizn vperedi, slushai sovieti druziei* [Lena, go forward in your creative endeavors, listen to the advice of your friends."]

The inscription and the gift itself tell me a lot: my gift is the most valuable. The inscription says that he appreciates my worth. First of all, a creative career awaits me; that is, I have a vocation. Second,

---

* Isaak Levitan, noted Russian-Jewish painter.
† A play on words—*Gorky* means "bitter" in Russian.
‡ Shosta Rustaveli (1172–1216), Georgian poet.

he considers himself one of my friends! But he understands that I don't appreciate his advice. That I didn't pay attention to or take to heart what he has said till now. I feel a surge of strength and energy. A creative career awaits me. Which one?

Saturday the 6th of December [1941], 9:00 in the morning (during a free period in school)

Yesterday in school we had an evening devoted to the anniversary of the Stalin Constitution [of 1936]. I recited Mayakowski's two poems "The Poem About the Soviet Passport" and "The Ten-Year-Old Poem." Despite the fact that I haven't recited for a long time, it went well. I spoke with passion and made an impression. A few days ago I had a very serious discussion with one of my classmates. For the last two days I've been feeling the impact of her words. She told me about her love affair with our Constitution teacher. She told me how she always tried to be where he could see her, tried to draw his attention to her. At first he didn't notice, and she was dejected. Later they became friends, drew very close. They used to meet every day in the doctor's office, where she would lie in his arms. He kissed her, petted her, and fondled her breast, talking to her all the while. She loved him very much and felt happy. He demanded that she give herself to him. But she did not want to. So he tried to take her by force! She defended herself and was able to drive him away. By then their relations had already cooled. My friend's character and her constant impulse toward male conquests are becoming clear to me.

I am a person from quite a different background, and with a different character.

Wednesday the 10th of December [1941], 12:30 in the afternoon

I haven't been to school for several days because I've been sick and in bed. I had a fever. Now my fever is gone, but I still feel bad. Nevertheless, I got dressed. But something terrible has happened: overnight my eyeglasses disappeared! Sick as I was, I searched, overturned the bed, swept the room, all to no avail. I cried like never before: I've lost half the light of the world, in the literal sense of the term. For me the world is now dim when it's bright for everyone else; and dark when it's dim for others. I'm desperate! I've lost my parents, my friends, my home, my beliefs, even the light! What do I have left? I'm such an unlucky person. How will I study? How can I do anything at all—live? Everyone feels sorry, shows sympathy for me. I'm grateful to them all, but what good does it do me? A couple of days will pass, and they'll all forget about me, they'll go their way. But me? I'll continue to suffer, because it's impossible to find glasses for sale here. Tomorrow the director is going to Izhevsk, so I'll try to persuade him to take me along; maybe I can buy glasses there—though I strongly doubt it. "He" said that he looked for a pair for a friend and was told that there were none. Still, I will try to go. But I'm still sick, it seems: my back is aching.

Saturday the 13th of December [1941], 12:00 noon (during a drawing class)

The director did not take me along to Izhevsk. His reason was that the weather is very cold and I am still sick. But he promised to buy glasses for me if he can find a pair. I gather that he has some hope. What will I do? I go to school, but see absolutely nothing on the blackboard or on the map. I am miserable. I miss my home more than ever. My mother was right when she said that you long for home when you have a problem. The news from the front is more encouraging. The Germans have been driven back some on the western and southern fronts. America and Canada have declared war on Japan, because Japan has come out against England.* Maybe we can expect something good? When will the war finally be over? My life is hateful to me. The loss of my glasses

---

* On December 7, 1941, Japan bombed Pearl Harbor. The next day, America declared war on Japan. Canada and England followed suit.

has nearly done me in. Everyone is amazed at how they disappeared overnight. A few think that someone did it out of spite, or jealousy, to prevent me from studying. I doubt it, because I can't imagine who could have done it. After all, I'm liked by the whole group.

Wednesday the 17th of December [1941], 11:00 in the morning

The director telephoned from Izhevsk that there are no glasses to be had there either. I am miserable. It seems to me that my eyesight is getting weaker and more dim. What will happen? Will I become permanently blind? It horrifies me! I can't see the blackboard. But I study as before and get excellent evaluations. Yesterday began the courses for combine operators, which I was forced to take. I left during the break because I couldn't see the drawings on the board and understood nothing. I am dropping out; I won't study anymore.

Yesterday a terrible thing happened: a father, a refugee from Lithuania, arrived looking for his child in our group. And it turned out that his child was never with us, because he had been at the Palanga camp in Lithuania. The Palanga camp was located in an area where there was no railroad. When the war started, all the children set off on foot to the train. Some of them were picked up by Red Army men in trucks. Some were scattered about, and nobody knows what became of them. The father spent a lot of money on telegrams looking for his child, unfortunately to no avail. But he learned that in Sarapul there's a camp of children evacuated from Lithuania, and wrote us to ask if we have a little boy named Edelshtat from Lithuania.

Rebecca Izraelevna, the headmistress, thought that in the Lithuanian camp there was such a child, because she remembered hearing the name Edelshtat. But that's because we have a girl here from Bialystok named Edelshtat! For that reason she wrote to the father telling him to send a letter to Sharkan.[*] She would also write,

---

[*] The place where a Soviet office was located for the reuniting of families separated by the war.

so that he wouldn't lose contact with the child. Overjoyed and confident, the father came to see us and unfortunately did not find his child. The father departed brokenhearted and disappointed. All the while he bitterly denounced the Soviet authorities, their bureaucracy and negligence. I can imagine the father's pain. He said that he'd been unwilling to remarry, so that his four-year-old would not have a stepmother. He sacrificed everything for his child, and now . . . That's war for you!

Who knows how it pains my mother to look for me, how hard it is for her to live through! Poor Mama! Don't cry over me and don't look for me. It's a waste of your tears. I am alive!

From the front there is encouraging news: we have recaptured Kalinin. The mood is better than before. There are greater hopes for victory. Perhaps?

Thursday the 18th of December [1941], 3:00 in the afternoon

Every day I better understand life and people. At home I would have remained the same naïve romantic. Here in the children's home I see only a part of what's going on in this country. The cook and the custodian steal food. The director's sister and her daughter live with us and eat with us, though it's not official. At first I believed that the cook loved our children and also her work. Unfortunately, I've become convinced that she does not. She screams at the children, steals butter and sausage from the kitchen. The director pampers her—kisses, pets her. She sells him her love, has already lain in his arms a few times. Just because it's in her interest—even though it's all dishonest. Now I understand why "he" used to make remarks to me. He understood that he doesn't matter to me. I never want to be like them. I want to be pure and honest in the deepest and broadest sense of the word.

I think: what will happen, when the war is over? Where will I go? Perhaps with Fanny P. and Shura to Leningrad? They seriously proposed it to me. I no longer have any hope of seeing my parents again.

Saturday the 20th of December [1941], 1:00 in the afternoon (during drawing class)

Volodya has given me two photographs of himself. He came out very handsome. From the picture two shining, lively eyes look out at you, his passionate lips laugh, revealing beautiful white teeth. His face and figure are manly and heroic. For a long time I couldn't tear my eyes away from the photo. I do not love Volodya, I don't even feel the slightest sympathy for him, because he's shallow, frivolous, and foolish. I'm only attracted and charmed by his photograph. I seek an ideal that I cannot find. I want to fall in love, but I have no one to fall in love with. I like Volodya's external appearance, but I am repelled by his inner nature.

Sunday the 21st of December [1941], 7:00 in the evening

Today was a happy day for me: I got up in a good mood. Because last night at a school function I performed Mayakowski's "Passport" and "Ten-Year Old Poem." I made a very good impression. Pyotr Andreyevich, the literature teacher, and Nina Nikolaevna, the chemistry teacher, were delighted. Afterward I danced a lot and watched the local dances.

Second, the Young Pioneer parade at the children's home, which at my initiative has been scheduled for Sunday mornings, went very well. Third, my Russian homework for tomorrow turned out very well. So, I'm enjoying myself!

Finally—the most important thing. The director returned from Izhevsk and brought me back glasses. True, they're not as good as mine were. Maybe a slightly different strength? But still, I see a lot better with them than without them. "He" told me that they were very hard to get (I can believe that). He got them through the military commander, because all optical glasses are the property of the armed forces. He brought two pairs of glasses. One pair is no good at all. I took the second. Now I'm happy! I thanked him warmly and asked him how I could repay him. "He" was touched and told me to continue to study hard. But that's what I do anyway, and for myself!

Genya and Lena, December 19, 1941

Thursday the 25th of December [1941], 3:00 in the afternoon

A few days ago Genya and I had our pictures taken. Today we picked up the photographs. How old we look! Have we really changed so much since that terrible day when we left home? Why did the photograph surprise me so much, more than our images in the mirror? I have truly changed. I am ashamed to say it, but sometimes I think in Russian—against my will. Now, for example, I wanted to inscribe my picture, and automatically inscribed it in Russian. Genya noticed and was astonished. She asked me why I wrote in Russian. She still writes in Polish. I couldn't answer her sudden question. I can barely give myself an answer: my half year of living in such a Russian environment, the absence of Jewish cultural life—have brought about these sad results. Maybe I'll soon forget how I once was, what Leyke looked like.

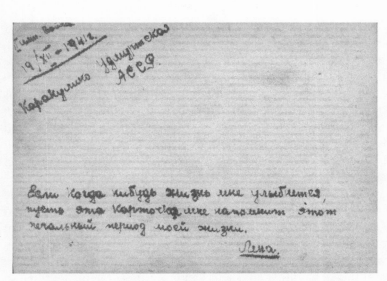

Lena's inscription on the back of the December 19, 1941 photograph:
If life ever smiles at me, let this photograph remind me of this sad
period in my life.

Lena

Friday the 26th of December [1941], 10:00 in the evening

For a long time I've wanted to write about Shura, my
classmate, the daughter of Fanny P. She is sixteen and a half years
old, with a delicate, pale countenance and two nearsighted green
eyes that look lost in thought and poetic. Her hair is dark, though
lighter than mine, plaited into two braids that reach down to her
waist. My first encounter with her was in Sarapul. We met in
school there and became friends. At that time her mother wasn't
yet working at the children's home, but I already knew that she
was Samuil Markovich's* cousin. Shura told me that they come
from Leningrad, that she'd been an excellent student, that she was
tutored privately in German, a little bit in English, and especially in
music—in piano. She truly played beautifully!

* Samuil Markovich Pevzner, director of the children's home in Karakulino.

49

Although I had never studied music, I still understood how much feeling there was in her performance. I was very pleased with my new acquaintance. I hoped to find in her an intelligent, sensitive girl, with a deep nature, a poetic soul, and great talent. In Sarapul I couldn't yet tell how well she learned, because she was mostly ill. Nevertheless I noticed that she studied a lot, but didn't understand physics and mathematics. As it was, I always helped her. Now that we're living together in Karakulino, I got to know her better. She's often "sick" with a fever of 37° C [98.6° F]. After two weeks of "sickness," she goes to school for four days and gets "sick" again. She feels that she cannot remember things, even when she studies hard. She becomes irritable, screams at her mother, and gets "sick." She envies me because I always have time and can memorize well. Earlier, when I didn't have all my schoolbooks, she was reluctant to lend me hers, out of jealousy. I quarreled with her over that. She thinks she's a real genius, a great talent. I offered to help with her homework assignments, teach her how to do them systematically. But she turned me down, saying, "I have a good memory, I'm capable in general, I can cope brilliantly by myself!" She considers me a close friend; why doesn't she trust me? All in all, she is very one-dimensional. Even in Leningrad, she tells me, she never went anywhere—seldom to the movies, or the theater, always at home with her lessons. In her own words, she doesn't feel the loneliness and gloom of Karakulino, because her intellectual life was no more colorful even in Leningrad. She is naïve, foolish. Her mother is fully aware of her negative thoughts, how exceptionally inept she is, how unsuited she is for life. She worries a lot about her and remains silent, though she suffers a great deal. When Shura studies until two o'clock in the morning and still hasn't memorized the material her mother has prepared for her, she worries that she still does not know the subject matter. But, in fact, Shura doesn't really study; she yells at her mother and makes scenes. Fanny P. has asked me several times to study with her, to calm her down and convince her that she'll know the material and answer well in class. Because I like Fanny P. and think highly of her, I help Shura and remain friends with her. I have no feelings for her, but I feel sorry for her mother: a daughter like that is simply a punishment. She's a *shlimazel*, a ne'er-do-well, but she's luckier than me. She has an educated mother who understands her, takes good care of her, has provided her with a brilliant education and cultural environment. She is deeply loved and nurtured. And what about me? Fate has endowed her with good fortune. Why did it punish me, rob me of my parents?

Saturday the 27th of December [1941], 12:00 noon

The disaster I dreaded has happened! With horror I write down this sad fact. Yes, I've caught the nasty, filthy disease that's infected many of us here. I have scabies. On a small part of my body there appeared little pimples, which harbor microscopically small, ugly little parasites, that dig into my skin and eat away at my tissues. It is horribly painful, especially at night. The one bit of good luck in my bad luck is that they haven't yet succeeded in spreading across my entire body, only on the upper part of my right leg and a bit of my stomach. The rest of my body is clean. For several days I hesitated to go to the doctor because I was ashamed. But yesterday I finally went. She verified the onset of the sickness and told me to smear on a special black ointment for three days. It's a secret I keep from everyone, except Genya. I feel so broken, humiliated, spiritually crushed—and I can't reveal my misfortune to anyone. Despite the fact that almost everybody has already come down with it, a daily occurrence with us, I still cannot calm down. I don't need to be isolated, because with a mild form of the disease I can't infect anyone.

This morning I experienced some especially painful moments. I applied the ointment so that nobody would notice. But the sharp odor, familiar to all, carried across the entire room and betrayed me. Everyone started to look around to see where the smell was coming from, who was using the ointment. I was miserable and cowardly—I kept silent. Genya helped me a lot. When they all approached my bed, lamp in hand, she turned their attention to another corner. How grateful I am to her for that! At the same time, I'm still very miserable. How will I be able to smear on the ointment—today, tomorrow, and the day after tomorrow? Sooner or later they'll discover the sad, painful secret. What will be then? My sheet has two fat brown stains, my clothes are dirty, and I myself—the same. I'd like to run away somewhere, to flee from my own skin. My self-esteem is crushed, soiled, my heart aches.

Wednesday the 31st of December [1941], 12:00 noon (during a literature class)

There's a real mess involving the Living Newspaper.* The director has latched onto my jokes, which everyone agrees are clever and funny, and has refused to let them pass under the pretext that they're counterrevolutionary. When I compare our dining room somewhat to hell; when I say that a notebook is a collection of solo-flying pages, covered with hieroglyphics, stains, and bad opinions; that grammar is a good sleeping pill, he considers it an insult to the entire group. He proposes instead to list the names of the poor students. Of course, I totally disagree. I explained that it wouldn't provoke laughter, but anger, on the part of everyone. I wouldn't want to look at it. For that reason, "he" was very angry with me yesterday, yelled at me and called me deficient in Communist education, a coward. Fanny P. came to my defense, and he yelled at her. Some of the girls know about it. Among us "he" has no other name than "despot," "tyrant," and "narrow-minded idiot." Everybody is very angry with him. Fanny P. told me this morning that I should read out the newspaper anyway, just not the part that's been censored, because otherwise I'll draw his wrath down on me. Of course, this way he'll love me.

Fanny P., Berta P., Rebecca Izraelevna, and Helena Pantelemonovna (the instructors in arts and crafts) later expressed their sympathy and admiration. Everyone is on my side, and against him. I have no idea yet what awaits me this evening.

---

* Current events in the form of skits, and the like.

My illness is not yet over. My hope that, along with the old year, which has brought me so much trouble and suffering, the wretched illness would also come to an end has evaporated. Last night I washed myself and put on clean underwear. During the night I was in great pain and had to apply more ointment. When will I be rid of this hateful plague?

Yesterday I sat with Shura on the top floor and did my homework. Volodya came over and began to pick on us. He spread me out on the floor and bent my arms behind my back. He stood bent over me. My blood caught fire. His physical beauty and strength aroused my passions; several minutes after he left I still hadn't recovered. Then I reminded myself how silly, shallow, and frivolous he is, and I became indifferent. I even smiled disparagingly.

Thursday the 1st of January [1942], 11:00 in the morning

New Year's Day! How much joy, hope, and surprise are connected with this day. The first day of the new year 1942. Before me lie great mysteries and expectations. What will this year bring? Where does my path lead, where will I be stranded? The old year, which I awaited a year ago full of expectations, brought me misfortune. On the sixteenth of June, a period of my life—my home, my parents, my friends—ended forever. On the sixteenth of June I left Bialystok an enthusiast, a naïve dreamer, who looked at life through rose-colored glasses, who believed fully in humane honesty and sincerity. The second half of the old year has taught me a lot; I've undergone a total metamorphosis. I perceived what life had to show me, things that couldn't be covered over by the earlier ready-made phrases. During this time I've grown up and grown three times older. What does the new year have in store for me? A breakthrough on the front? The fact that our divisions have gone over to the offensive, that we have recaptured Tikhvin, Rostov, Kerch, and Feodosia[*] inspires great hopes! Perhaps. In my fantasy I see Mama, Papa, those dearest to me. Who knows? The prospects

---

[*] Tikhvin is near Leningrad, the other towns are in southern Russia and the Crimea.

are very dim. Yesterday we had a New Year's Eve celebration. I didn't perform the Living Newspaper. We had a beautiful program. I acted in a play and was a big hit. I was able to evoke and to embody a character. The atmosphere was very good. I invited two girls from our class, who unfortunately were a burden to me, because I had to drag them along with me the whole time, since Shura would quickly disappear.

I was very touched yesterday by Rebecca Izraelevna. Despite the fact that it was she who, in effect, arranged the evening, who trimmed the New Year's tree,[*] prepared the newspaper and the costumes, she wasn't given a place at the guest table. Only later was she called over. After midnight Genya and I called on her to wish her a happy New Year. She was touched, and she cried and thanked us.

I cried myself. Genya sobbed. As soon as Rebecca Izraelevna had left, Genya burst out laughing at her expense. I was furious at her falseness, and told her that she was a brilliant actress. How can a person be so false? For reasons of convenience to deceive, flatter, express sympathy, and a second later—to ridicule! That is the face of a snake. How can I find a common language with her? Who knows what she thinks of me and writes in her diary? I no longer can trust her. She is base, and I despise her.

Friday the 2nd of January [1942], 10:00 in the morning

Volodya has taken to drinking. He is inexperienced at it and becomes terribly pale and drowsy. He disgusts me, this good-looking apple that's healthy on the outside, but rotten and wormy on the inside. Last night he and Viktor[†] Severukhin a student in our class, his best friend, invited Genya and me to the club for a performance. Viktor is a tall, healthy seventeen-year-old youth, with a manly build and a heroic countenance. A poor student, but quite a good artist. On the way it became clear that they had both been drinking wine, with the difference that Viktor wasn't drunk, but

---

[*] In the Soviet Union, whose leaders rejected religious symbolism, the popular tradition of trimming Christmas trees was permitted to continue in the guise of calling them New Year's trees.

[†] In subsequent entries, his first name is given as Vitaly.

Volodya couldn't stand on his feet! Viktor told me, while under the influence, about his childhood. Now, as it turns out, he's in trouble. During a performance, instead of putting on a wooden stiletto, he put on a metal Finnish dagger. Someone accidentally fell on it and was wounded in the foot. Viktor was held legally at fault and faces five years' imprisonment. He is desperate, his parents even more so. He submitted a plea to the court to be allowed to volunteer for the army. If all goes well—that is, if he only has to pay a fine—he'll go directly to the front. What prompted him to sacrifice his young life, I asked him. Because I know that he is no *komsomolets* [member of the Young Communist League] and not even much of a patriot. He answered that he was sick of it all. He began to tell me about his childhood: he was born in Sverdlovsk to well-to-do parents, but he had bad friends. He became the leader of a gang of thieves at the age of twelve. They were in Moscow, Leningrad, Ukraine; they stole and went to prison for three months several times. At age fifteen, he went back home.

What should I think about him now? Maybe he's in exile here on account of all that? What should I think about his story? An "artist"? I understand why he's demoralized. He stays on his feet pretty well after drinking, he plays cards, smokes. Quite a negative image, one would think. And yet he has traits that arouse your sympathy. He is quite intelligent, and knowing that he is a nobody, he respects and appreciates people who are superior. In good company he is well behaved. He is kind by nature: for example he gave me some photographic plates to take my picture with, something that you simply cannot get here. Yesterday, in a fatherly way, he looked after Volodya, who couldn't stand on his feet. He put him to bed, indulged him in everything he asked, got him a place at the club. Human nature is so complicated. Who can fathom someone else's personality?

Saturday the 3rd of January [1942], 11:00 in the morning

This morning Fanny P. called me aside, saying she had to talk to me about something. She came out of the kitchen where she was on duty and asked me to help her solve a certain problem. I surmised that it involved Shura! Naturally, I promised I would help. With tears in her eyes she told me that it's very hard for her, that she's going through a lot, that she has no time for her daughter, who needs it more than anything. Shura is in poor health. She is used to doing her homework conscientiously, but here she realizes that it's too hard for her. She cannot cope; she feels that she's not achieving her goals, and as a result she's terribly nervous. She has become dull and indifferent to life. She is desperate and despairing and has a pessimistic outlook. She is ready to give up studying—everything.

I was very moved by Shura's condition. I was moved even more by her mother—Fanny P.—than by Shura. She is an intelligent woman, a lawyer by profession, who is very devoted to our children's home. She surrounds all the children with motherly care, including Genya and me. She has asked me to help Shura; she even wept on my shoulder. Because she devotes all her time to other people's children, to those who no longer have parents, she has no time for her own daughter. She has no space of her own; she and her daughter are stuck in the attic at Samuil Markovich's. Even though her sister, B. P., has rented a room where they'll soon move, three people in a room cannot compare with a six-room apartment in Leningrad. Meanwhile, they have seen to it that Shura doesn't have to run to us for breakfast, lunch, and supper. They take pains that I shouldn't be far away because Shura would then be unable to ask me to help her with what she doesn't understand. Now I see how life has broken people—not Shura, but her mother. I am greatly moved by the despair of this intelligent, kind woman. I assured her that I will help in any way I can. I could not express what I felt and experienced. How I love her! An unhappy mother, who has raised a helpless child. She's been like a mother to me, and many times she told me, seriously, that when the war ends I can go with them to Leningrad if I cannot go home. She wants to create a homey space for me in her nest. Materially, she can afford it. Her husband is a chief engineer at a Leningrad concern. All in all, they come from an established, well-educated family of engineers, the old-style intelligentsia of the past.

Monday the 5th of January [1942], 12:00 noon

Vladimir Alexandrovich has just announced that on the eighteenth of this month the second quarter will come to an end. There will be no vacation. The third, and last, quarter starts right away. It will probably end in April when the planting campaign begins. We will be sent to the fields. Still, they're trying to complete the curriculum. It's not yet known when we'll be examined.

I've grown closer to Shura. Yesterday I explained physics, algebra, and trigonometry to her. Afterward she studied the entire day. In the evening, till three o'clock in the morning—literature. All day I read Dobrolyubov's critical articles on Ostrovsky's works, and didn't even pick up a textbook. When we were both called on in class, both of us got "excellent." Shura was amazed and called me a "genius." She greatly exaggerates my abilities, because studying is so hard for her. Her mother thanked me today for spending the whole day with her. Yesterday Shura was more cheerful than usual, and even ate normally. Fanny P. was simply delighted.

Tomorrow there will be a test in chemistry class. For that reason I have to sit and study all day with Shura. This work that I have taken on myself costs me a lot of time, which I could use for reading, but, after all, I have to express my gratitude to Fanny P. It gives me pleasure when Shura knows the correct answers and feels cheerful, and especially when Fanny P., happy and radiant, comes to see how we are doing.

Wednesday the 7th of January [1942], 11:00 in the morning

Shura is causing me grief. She studied all day and all night, till five o'clock in the morning. That day she did not go to school and didn't take either of the tests in geometry and chemistry. Then she studied until six in the evening and went to school to meet with the teacher, Nina Nikolaevna, in order to answer the chemistry questions. Nina Nikolaevna was by then no longer in school. Today she wants to go to her home. She is absent from school again, because today she was supposed to answer questions on Darwinism and take a test in Russian literature. I feel terribly sorry for her, because she is truly an unhappy, dull girl.

Now we're preparing a play with Helena Pantelemonovna, *Svyerkaitye Almazy* [Sparkle, Diamonds]. Six girls and nine boys are to participate. The main characters are Lida and Vladek. Since there are few boys among us, I will invite Vitaly Severukhin to play the male lead. I hope he'll agree to do it; he's played this part a few times before. I will play Lida. I want to play opposite him because he's a good actor, despite his various negative traits. Today we'll read from the text in front of the drama circle.

Saturday the 10th of January [1942], 3:00 in the afternoon

I've become very used to my situation and way of life here, since, after all, I have no alternative. Last night, when I was at Asya's for supper, the school's Pioneer leader, a Jewish girl from Moscow, Fira Alotina, was also present. She was evacuated from Moscow along with her parents, her sister, and her sister's child. Together with us she had some bread, sour cheese, tea with sugar. She ate quietly and slowly. When we had finished eating, she took half her supper for her nephew. We were very moved. We had a sense of what hunger looks like there. Three people are working in their home and they can't even support a child! Here everything is so expensive: butter costs 60 rubles a kilo, meat 70 rubles—that's why it's so hard to get. And that's in a country village, so what happens in the city? We get 400 grams of bread per person per day. We work hard under difficult conditions, especially for refugees, and still there is no food.

Today Fira came for lunch, ostensibly to visit Asya. I called her over to our table, and we all ate together. That was certainly a happy, fulfilling day for her!

I remembered what people said about the first years of the Soviet Union. I've read a lot about the starvation during that time: people perished, parents ate their own children—there actually were such cases! Now, with the first year of war still not over, we face a similar situation. What will happen if the war drags on?

I'm beginning to believe that I have a star in heaven that guides me in life and preserves me from misfortune. Now I find myself in a children's home where I am fed, I study, I have a warm room, sleep in a bed! I am appreciated by all the children, the instructors, and teachers. It's a pleasure to be able to study, to profit from the sources of knowledge at least to a limited extent, since books aren't available here—but still!

Fanny P. and B. P. are seriously considering the idea that if the war ends and it's not possible for us to return home, they will take me and Genya along to their home in Leningrad.

Things are going well for me. But what about my family and close friends in Bialystok? They are persecuted and tortured, they starve and suffer greatly. Fate has spared me! I lack only a guide to show me in which direction to develop myself. To this day I don't know what interests me more: mathematics and physics, or literature, languages, and history. What should I be, an engineer, a teacher, a writer, or an actress? Maybe for the time being I ought to make no plans at all, since we don't know yet when and how the war will end.

Sunday the 11th of January [1942], 2:00 in the afternoon

"Mich träumt ich weiss nicht was [I long for I know not what]."

—Heine

I am sad, I yearn, I ponder, I want . . . what? I myself don't know.

Life is tedious, trivial, gray. Days go by, I live with petty, everyday cares. Every day I get up at seven-thirty, wash, brush my teeth, comb my hair, make the bed, eat breakfast, and go to school, which is located 20 to 25 meters away. Four, five hours in school and then—back here. Lunch, and then again—lectures, classroom assignments, books. I still have free time. I chatter, think, and am bored. From time to time I'm the monitor in our dormitory and dining hall. Once every two weeks I chair the children's council, reviewing the work of the committees. Sundays I lead the Young Pioneer parade. The day off puts me in a bad mood and is tedious. What's pleasant are the three times a week when the drama circle meets for three hours. For the time being I have no goal in life whatsoever. More and more I'm losing my former personality and I cannot imagine my future. I want the war to end as quickly as possible. What's waiting for me then?

Wednesday the 14th of January [1942], 4:00 in the afternoon

I've already done all my homework, and soon I will start reading. What? I don't even know. After all, I don't have any books yet. I have a sore throat. Maybe I should go to bed . . . but I don't want to sleep. If I go to sleep now, I won't be able to sleep at night. I'm in a bad mood! I want to get rid of it, but I can't. I feel a weakness, and I can't do anything except write in my diary. My diary is my most intimate friend! Only to my diary do I entrust my thoughts and my secrets, pour out my heart, seek consolation. My paper friend, you are part of my being. I hope that you won't betray me because you are in Yiddish and few here can read it. And from those that can read it, I can hide it well!

Friday the 16th of January [1942]

Yesterday, the fifteenth of January, was the sixteenth birthday of my close friend Sorele Davidovsky. Last year I was at your fifteenth birthday celebration. This year I cannot even send you a greeting. But I love you very much; our friendship was always an ideal one, the envy of many of our acquaintances. Who knows if we'll ever meet again? Who knows where you are now? Dear, loving, Sorele, will we forget each other over time? For the time being I have to make new friends. You, too. In that respect you're luckier than me, because you're living in our environment. Perhaps I haven't yet been forgotten. You know, Sorele, I may be luckier than you. I am still studying. And you? Are you already working in the factory with your mother? Are you suffering from hunger? Are you alive? I tremble for your fate! How is your mother? I love her as much as my own mother. All the best to you!

Now my best friend is Genya. But we have different personalities, not like with you. Our friendship stems from our material circumstances and from our shared fate, having lost our homes and families. We are both lonely and deprived of our milieu.

Sunday the 18th of January [1942], 4:00 in the afternoon

Genya moved out of our room yesterday and went to sleep at Tanya's. They've again become as close as they were in Sarapul. In the morning I was in a bad mood on account of that: I felt sad and lonely. In addition, I still had a sore throat and was coughing very hard. I decided to stay in bed and even had breakfast there. As time passed, my restlessness increased and I felt lonely. So I dressed quickly. But the day was unpleasant. I'm not at ease with myself: I don't read, I'm not studying my part in the play, I feel that all is not well with me. What's more, I need a close friend more than ever!

Monday the 19th of January [1942], 1:00 in the afternoon

Today we have a 40-degree frost [-40° C] and nobody went to school. I woke up in a deep gloom. I had a sad dream: I thought that I was coming home from someplace far away and I found nobody there. Uncle Pinchas tells me that Mama and Papa tried to go to Grodno* as soon as the war broke out. Papa broke his foot along the way. There is no other news of them. Later I apparently did meet Mama, but I didn't see Papa anywhere. I sat with Mama at home and cried. Then a German soldier came and started to beat

* A city in prewar Poland (now in Belarus) 50 miles northeast of Bialystok.

me. Afterward I fled to the trenches and was pelted with stones. In this manner the dream reminded me of my home and family! Who knows if they are alive and how they live? Only Papa is fit for work. Moyshl's health is quite poor and he is fifteen years old. Did they survive the bombardment, the tortures of the German occupation? They certainly must be suffering from hunger. Maybe our house has collapsed? How is my little thirteen-year-old sister Sorele? Moyshl no doubt is already working with Papa. How is Mama, how is her health? What are they thinking about me? Do they know that our camp was evacuated? Or do they think that the Germans deported us and they're grieving for me? On the radio I just heard a news broadcast. They said that we should expect a great deal from next spring. This war, which has enveloped the whole earth, has now reached its zenith with the entry of Japan and America. What change will that bring in our lives? Will it bring our return home, the reunion with loved ones, any closer?

It's more than eight months since we left our home, and eight months since the war started. But to me it seems much longer!

Friday the 23rd of January [1942], 1:00 in the afternoon

This entire week there have been big frosts: -48°, -52° [C] and we don't go to school. In school, by the way, there is no wood for heating. Usually they have to go to the woods to chop down trees, but now, because of the cold, it is impossible. The day before yesterday when I was in Tanya's room, I fell off her stool as I was warming myself by the stove. I hurt my legs badly: bloodied my left leg and injured the right knee, which is badly swollen. I fell onto the bed and bit my lips in pain. But I did not cry. Volodya, who was also in the room, took my fall very much to heart. He ran out and brought some snow and rubbed my legs. Then he went to his sister's, brought cotton and a bandage and applied two compresses. Because he showed me a lot of care and assistance, I was very touched. Now I've already removed the compresses. Yesterday, I was still limping a little; today I'm not, but it still hurts.

I'm not pleased with the "vacation" that nature has arranged for us. Days go by in idleness. I can't even do any schoolwork. I tried to prepare my lecture and had to stop right away on account of the pain. I couldn't even concentrate enough to learn the lines of the part that I'm supposed to play. I am not pleased with myself! Yesterday I spoke with Helena Pantelemonovna about my part. She said that I act very well. She thinks that I can look forward to a future on the stage, that I am talented, but need to work on myself. I'm very pleased with her opinion, but I want to be on the Yiddish stage, because that's closest to my heart.

Last night I and other girls from the children's home—Sima, Beyle, Basha, Vera, Chanele Lin (my sister Sorele's girlfriend)—began to sing Yiddish songs: revolutionary songs, folk songs, children's songs. It gave me great pleasure: we were carried back to our world, to our own culture.

Saturday the 24th of January [1942], 3:30 in the afternoon

Last night I went to the club with Genya, Volodya, and Vitaly. Genya and Volodya went ahead, Vitaly and I walking behind them. We spoke about the play and about Vitaly's trial, which is supposed to take place soon. In the club, Vitaly left us. On the way back there were only the three of us: Genya, Volodya, and I. When we got home, Genya told me that she's in love with Volodya. She added that she cannot tell Tanya, because to her, no one could compare with Pevzner. Genya asked me, if I wasn't jealous of her? Did I like Volodya? "No!" I told her. She was astonished and told me that I'm very kind! I was pleased: Genya and Volodya think highly of me, they're not ill at ease with me, keep no secrets from me. I follow their childish, naïve love affair. They're now both very nice. Thanks to this emotion, I think, Genya has somewhat raised herself to a higher level. What will I look like when I fall in love? But when will I find a comrade who is sensitive, a deep thinker, refined, bold, and wise? It's been a long time since I met someone with whom I could have an interesting conversation. If I meet someone like that, perhaps I, too, will fall in love.

At times I look around. Where I find myself there are so many different personalities with particular characteristics. Each has its own nature, its specific qualities and traits. More than anyone else, I like Vera Furmanski. She is sixteen years old and in the seventh grade. She is a Warsaw girl. When the Germans entered Warsaw, she and her older brother came to us in Bialystok. They lived as refugees, and then she became very ill and lay in the hospital for two years. Now she has a very weak heart and tuberculosis. While she was lying in the hospital, her brother was drafted into the Red Army. So she remained alone and very lonely. The two years in the hospital have left very visible traces. In terms of her health, she's already half an invalid, and in terms of her character, a young pessimist. After leaving the hospital she was settled in a children's home. Because of her fragile health, and because she knew neither Russian nor Yiddish, she couldn't go to school. Her mother tongue is Polish. Last summer she came to the Pioneer camp in Druskenik, which is why she is with us now. Vera is intelligent, well read, clever. Since she finds herself among healthy people, she sometimes forgets about her illnes and is filled with good cheer and happiness. Unfortunately her body often reminds her that she's sick: she experiences pain. But she does not complain. Vera inspires respect. I like to talk to her, have discussions; I admire her! She's heard something about my past from girls who know me from the Yiddish schools; she admires me. At times she criticizes my behavior, just as I do hers. It never bothers me, because I consider her an honorable person. Vera is capable, serious; she thinks about her future, and wants to study further to master science. But she doubts whether she'll succeed, whether her health will hold out. Last night she suddenly began to talk about it and ended on a sad note: "I feel that I won't even be able to finish the seventh grade in peace," she said. "It cannot be, it's too big a stroke of luck for me, will it even be possible?" I said to her: "Why are you such a pessimist, Vera? You're so unhappy, a pity! Your abilities, your intellect, and cleverness promise a lot! Maybe all is not lost concerning your health, maybe your youth will overcome your illness and you'll be the victor, God willing!"

I am also close to Galya Mazo, a tall, slender girl with long black braids and brown eyes. She is sixteen years old and in the eighth grade. Her father is a pediatrician; he was my teacher in grade school. Her mother is a dental technician. Galya is their only child. At home she had her own room, where she did her homework, read, listened to the radio. She used to have supper in the evening with her parents, listening to their discussions. All in all, she was surrounded with much care and love. Raised in a well-to-do, intelligent family, she had little experience of life, was able to realize all her childhood dreams. Now she is greatly changed. At first she stood aside from the group and withdrew into herself. Lately she's come closer, has become a member of the children's council and the school committee. Galya is dignified, well brought up, deep. It was harder for her than for anyone else to get used to conditions at the children's home. The sharp contrast between her cozy little room in her parents' home and our communal dormitory at the children's home—filled with people rushing about, noise, and sometimes quarreling—disturbed her. Now she's become acquainted with children from our social background and has grown used to it. She even admires me. She let me read her diary, in which she describes her experiences. Galya is very shy, not bold. I see in her a serious, responsible, not at all frivolous person. She likes to observe her environment and draw her own conclusions. She'll probably develop into an honest, serious member of society.

Sunday the 25th of January [1942], 5:30 in the evening

Today we went to a concert. There were performances by members of the Udmurtian[*] State Theater—songs and dances. It was very beautiful, even better than we had expected. We expressed our wish to have concerts like that more often!

At the children's home ugly things are happening. Because our bread ration has been cut again (to 400 grams a day), because for a

[*] Karakulino was located in the Udmurtian ASSR. Udmurtian, a Finno-Ugric language, is spoken by some sixty thousand people.

long time we've had no meat at dinner,[*] and no kasha[†] either, just a little cabbage, always just cabbage. So all the kids are hungry lately. Everybody is depressed and dreams of one more piece of bread, but none is to be had. Some people trade the portions of sugar or butter that they get with their bread to the younger children for an additional piece of bread. When the counselors found out about it, they called a general meeting and denounced the behavior. Unfortunately, it hasn't stopped. Boys in the fifth and sixth grades continue to do it, and even some seventh grade girls. A member of the Housekeeping Committee, who is on duty in the kitchen two days a week handing out the food, takes a double portion for herself. She doles out more bread to those with whom she's on good terms—she gives more bread to the seventh grade! At the table, when people see an extra portion, one person grabs the bread, another, the butter and sugar. It's always that way. Those who are brazen and quick always have more and don't suffer from hunger. Those who are quiet and shy are constantly hungry. This morning there was an interesting situation at breakfast: Sima was monitor in the dining hall, Basha in the kitchen. When Sima handed out the portions, it turned out that everybody had two small slices of bread; Sima and Basha—three apiece. All the kids noticed, but nobody said a word. Somebody asked if they might not get a supplement, another slice of bread. Sima went off to inquire and, after a few minutes, came back with two slices of bread. Somebody asked for half a slice. But she did not give it up. Instead, she divided it between herself and Basha! This greatly upset everybody. We decided that she is an egotist.

When Basha came into the dining hall and saw that she had four slices of bread and everybody else only two, she was ashamed and generously offered somebody a slice. Nobody would take it, because, after all, it's unfair. I told her to give it back to Sima! They all agreed with me. When Sima came in and saw her five slices of bread, she understood the meaning of this demonstration: she had

[*] *Mitog*: literally, midday meal.
[†] Kasha is a staple cereal, made of buckwheat.

put down four slices herself and we had added the fifth. Haughtily she said, "Thank you"! She tossed away one piece of bread, but nobody would touch it!

A similar story took place at dinner. She carried two portions of bread into the dormitory instead of the dining hall, and put them on her bed. All the girls in the room saw it and talked about it among themselves. It greatly angered me and I made a scene! Is this what you call cooperative, decent relationships? Why do you tear a bit of food out of others' mouths in order to satisfy your own hunger? Whoever is more brazen, aggressive, and vulgar always wins.

Vera supported me and told me that Sima still has reserves of snacks and sugar from Sarapul; that there, too, she used to grab extra portions! All the kids tend to strongly dislike Sima for her character; she's a certain type of person. I don't know her especially well, but I've heard about her past and I judge her by her behavior. This is my impression of her: she was born in Vilna and raised in a children's home. She says that her mother was a teacher there, but I don't know if that's true. All the kids say that she is a foundling!

She doesn't say much about her past. When I chide her for that, she tells me that her mother left for Palestine in 1939 and was supposed to bring her over when the war broke out! Then she fled to Bialystok and was placed in a children's home. There she was head of the children's council, a big shot. But everyone hated her and often rebelled against her. She flirted with one of the counselors and, thanks to that, gained various privileges. Those in our group who come from the same children's home, and who tell all sorts of amazing things about her, despise and yet fear her. Sima is smart, sly, not very talkative, and can adapt to any situation. She has a very high opinion of herself, thinks that she stands above every other girl in the seventh grade, makes fun of everybody, always distancing herself from the class. She maintains that nobody appreciates her abilities and that she's not given the role in society that she rightfully ought to occupy. She reproaches Genya and me for it, too. All the same, she learns from us: she knows that we read a lot and as a result have gained knowledge and everyone's respect. Therefore she's also started to read a lot, but unfortunately gets little out of it, since she's not perceptive, not bright. She has a strong personality: not easily influenced, independent, egotistical, impudent, coquettish with the boys, strong willed. What will she develop into? A petty bourgeois, a person who will defend her own interests and dominate all the weaker personalities. She already does it now.

It's a fact that Basha Reicher obeys her in everything. A lot of girls remain silent when she plays some dirty trick, because they don't want to hear the malicious, barbed sarcasm that pours out of her big mouth.

For society, for the collective, she doesn't want to do anything. For example, she carries out her responsibilities as a member of the children's council poorly. Sima represents the tyrant who has no possibility of sitting on the throne. That makes her even more malicious. We are the same age, though she is much shorter and looks younger. She pays no attention to what people say. She's so proud of her tough character. Such types are the enemies of humanity and *menschlichkeit*, humaneness. I despise them.

Monday the 26th of January [1942], 10:00 in the morning

Today the frost has let up a little: -23° C. Maybe tomorrow we can go to school, because the school is getting some firewood. I want to go to class already. I have a lot of time now, but I do nothing. Why? This is not the right atmosphere for work, not the right conditions. In the dormitory there's a lot of noise. None of the girls lifts a finger, they chatter, laugh, sing, or quarrel. When I'm in the room, they prevent me from doing anything. When I go away to Tanya's room, I can't do anything either, because they talk and laugh there as well. Right now I'm pretty disorganized. When I go to school my time is carefully structured and productive!

Yesterday evening I spoke with Rebecca Izraelevna about the past. I told her only one percent of my experiences. A funny thing! When I remember my childhood, everything seems so beautiful, interesting! What actually did I experience in the past? For three years I attended a charitable boarding school, where my little sister and I were fed. My brother stayed at another boarding school, because our parents couldn't feed us at the time. We were in the poorest stratum of society. I remember how I would go straight from school to TOZ[*] for the midday meal and stop by even for supper. Only at eight o'clock did I return home. That was in 1935 when I was in the fourth grade, ten years old. I suffered greatly then that I was so poor, and I felt ashamed.

I used to suffer most when, at Purim or New Year's, they would arrange evening performances for the women's philanthropic committee, and we would be trotted out on stage to recite and sing. Of course, there was a festive supper for the guests. They would bring cakes, apples, chocolate, cocoa. The audience would eat at richly provisioned tables, where you could see wine, oranges, chocolate, a variety of fruits, cakes, cookies. Naturally, we couldn't take our eyes away from these treats. But the apple and the piece of chocolate that we received we hid away for our families at home, in order to share this treasure.

I often would recite at these celebrations and bring these kindly ladies to tears. I understood that they pitied me, and it caused me pain. The ladies would also bring their children: attractive and well dressed, they would sit among the guests and observe us with interest. Sometimes I would think: Why do they deserve such a good life and I such a hard life?

I envied them and dreamed of being in their situation. Maybe I would find a treasure, bring good fortune to my mama, my papa, Sorele, and Moyshele, even all the children in the institution—the poor, the humiliated, the insulted! I was such a dreamer!

In the sixth grade I was already among the older girls, those who had been at the school for three years. By then I already understood that to earn a few privileges, to get something once in a while, you needed to get close to the authorities. But I didn't want to do it, and wasn't able to do it. The gang advised me: Do as we do! I obeyed them. We used to go down to the kitchen to help the cook wash and dry the dishes, peel potatoes, scrub carrots. In exchange,

[*] Abbreviation (Polish) for the Society for the Defense of Health, a Jewish children's charity in prewar Poland.

she would give us extra portions and ask the teacher to give us clothing that we needed. That helped a lot. I remember that in the sixth grade I never did any schoolwork between lunch and supper, because I spent whole days in the kitchen helping with the chores. I did my assignments when I was back at home. I looked very bad then, but I was happy since when there was bread left over at school, the cook would give it to us to take home. I felt so proud that I could bring a large loaf of bread home! Papa was unemployed then, so I could help him out materially a little. Mama used to thank me with a kiss!

In September of 1939 the German army arrived in Bialystok. It was a harsh occupation, as in all of Poland. Luckily, after seven days the Soviet army replaced the Germans. The economic situation was transformed. Papa stopped working at his trade and became a driver at a factory. He worked hard there, but earned little. So he didn't have even the barest necessities, like food. The question arose of my going to work. Since I still wanted to study, I kept at it, also continuing to give lessons to the poorer students. The money I earned, I gave to my mother, since she needed it. At the end of the 1940/1941 school year, I was sent from school to Pioneer summer camp at Druskenik.

Thereafter things got very interesting indeed: suddenly war broke out. They tried to send us back home, but it couldn't be done, since the railway line had been bombed and destroyed. We were evacuated, and after an eleven-day journey we were three thousand kilometers from home in Udmurtia, in Sarapul. After the Druskenik counselors left for home in the Soviet Union, Tanya, Genya, and I were selected as their temporary replacements. After three months in Sarapul, when new counselors were found, I began to return to school! A few days in Sarapul, and afterward in Karakulino, as a ward of the children's home, a student in the ninth grade!

The same day, 10:00 at night

Leise zieht durch mein Gemüht
Liebliches Geläute
Klinge, kleines Frühlingslied
Kling hinaus ins Weite.

—Heine

[Gently moving through my soul
A delightful ringing
Ring, little song of Spring
Ring out into the world.]

A wonderful play of feelings and impressions in my soul! Silken chords tremble, vibrate, create lovely, heartfelt tones that flow into a concerto of feeling. My ear listens to the tones that penetrate outward from within. My mood is sweet and warm, and I dream . . . of what? A peaceful picture of life is woven into the bluish haze of dreams. I see a well-ordered dwelling, a little room filled with books and light. You can feel the *heymishkayt* [coziness], pleasantness, warmth. I work on myself, study. Then I see my boyfriend, who is working beside me. We spend time together, converse. He is refined, clever, intelligent, deeply sensitive. We understand each other with our glances alone, we are close, we're united by a great, deep friendship. I see many good and pleasant things in my dream—everything that I lack in reality, that I long for. What a sharp contrast between reality and the dream! In fact I am very far from home, from my dearest loved ones. I am alone with my thoughts. I am living through a war that, with its ferocity, has brought grief to everyone. Thousands of people are killed at the front, thousands are tortured to death by the brown murderers.[*] A terrible hunger holds sway in our country: in Leningrad they've already eaten all the cats and dogs. They get 125 grams of bread a day, no fats or grains at all. Things are no better in the other cities. There rages a famine like the one in 1927.[†] This after eight months of war! What awaits us next?

---

[*] The Nazi Sturmabteilung (SA), or storm troopers, were also known as "brownshirts." "Brown" was used by anti-fascists to disparage Nazism as a whole.

[†] Possibly 1924? See the 4th of November, 1941 entry.

Who knows? I'm worried, I'm lacking so many things, although perhaps I am one of the lucky ones, since I have remained alive! But I have nowhere to channel my energy, my temperament. Will I ever be able to realize my aspirations and dreams?

Wednesday the 28th of January [1942]

Today classes resumed in school. I received the news happily, because I require work, variety. I have no classes today. All day tomorrow will be devoted to military preparedness. (I have no idea what the parts of a rifle or a grenade are called.) I've just read Paustovsky's *Levitan*[*] (the book was given to me for my birthday by Rebecca Izraelevna). The great artist's life was sad. You can see it from his thin face and dark, Jewish eyes. You also feel it when you look at his paintings.

Autumn—damp weather, a cold river, a gloomy forest, a bare shore. A shudder goes through all my limbs, I feel cold, and I get gooseflesh all over my body. A sadness in the soul.

Spring—a large body of water. Somewhat more cheerful colors. A body of water bordered by birches, a solitary fir tree, a leaden sky. Once again, cold, damp, severe.

In Eternal Rest—a quiet cemetery at the shore of a river, solitary crosses amid sparse fir trees, a remote church. It is night—dark, windy.

How do all these pictures conform to my present mood? A pain has settled into my heart, corroding one tissue after another, tangling my insides. An evil wind shakes my soul, and it trembles and flutters, torn by the wind. I reflect, I yearn, I want . . . to live to see the summer! I put great hopes on it. In my fantasy, my little sister's face flashed before me, with her black little eyes, rosy little cheeks, and pretty braids. My brother's face, his thick eyebrows and lashes! The Bialystok forest, the Doylida beach. Unwillingly, a sigh escapes from my breast . . . oh, it's hard!

---

[*] Isaak Levitan (1860–1900), noted Russian-Jewish painter, celebrated for his "landscapes of mood."

Jeruzalem, Jeruzalem, cudna ziemio Ty,
Gdy Twej mece nie poswiece kazdej mojej lzy,
Jesli Ciebie ne ogarne moim synowskim zalem,
To mnie preklnij i zapomnij, matko Jeruzalem!*

[If I forget thee, O Jerusalem, let my right hand wither!
Let my tongue cleave to the roof of my mouth,
if I do not remember you,
if I do not set Jerusalem above my highest joy!]

Thursday the 29th of January [1942], 6:00 in the evening

Today we had a full day of military preparedness. I didn't attend; I had a headache all day. Last year I dreamed of learning to fight, but today? What could I do in this condition?

In the afternoon I gave a talk about the work of the children's council. The work was judged to be satisfactory. The director of the children's home liked it. I am eager to do this work. I have a zest for it; the activity will be good for my mental state. I'll be able to discharge my energy and forget my pain. Every day I'll review something else, I'll collaborate with the other members of the council, and the work will go full steam ahead!

Saturday the 31st of January [1942], 10:00 at night

Today I won a victory for my part in the play. Helena Pantelemonovna, the actress, who selected us for the performance, and the others expressed their great appreciation. My role turned out very well! Yesterday I was at a very interesting lecture about the international situation. Rarely do you find such a good lecturer, especially in such an out-of-the way place as Karakulino! My mood has improved. I'm more hopeful, and things that I previously didn't understand have become clearer to me.

---

* Psalm 137:5–6 ("If I forget thee O Jerusalem") in a verse paraphase by the Polish poet Juliusz Slowacki.

Yesterday I had another run-in with the director: he told me to free my bed for a sick girl and to share a bed with somebody! I felt very hurt, but said nothing. Fortunately Shura ran to her mother, Fanny P., our supervisor, to tell her about it. Fanny P. intervened, and thanks to her, he rescinded the order. I am happy that I've found favor with the supervisors! It's no secret that Genya, Tanya, and I are privileged. After all, when the Druskenik counselors left, we took their places until new supervisors were found—nearly two months. That's why we have single beds, and have some authority. Fanny P. also looks after me because I'm Shura's friend and I help her. I'm very thankful to her for that and I love her.

Today in school they registered all students born in 1924 and 1925. Seven students in our class were sent away to work in Sarapul. I was afraid that I, too, would be mobilized. But my fear turned out to be baseless. I thought I was probably spared because I am an Honors student. Now I learn that I'm not being mobilized because I don't have good vision. It turns out that my misfortune is my good luck! From our children's home they'll probably send five boys to the military. Poor boys! Who knows how bitter things will be for them!

Everybody is already asleep in our room. You can hear them lightly snoring. The kerosene lamp burns feebly, the kerosene is giving out. I'll soon turn it off. But I won't go to sleep yet because the stove is still heating and I have to wait until I've warmed up.

Meanwhile, I think about home and my mother, who has already mourned for me. About Papa, my brother and little sister, about my friends. Have they forgotten me? For now, good night— till tomorrow! Then more monotonous gray days, weeks, months.

Monday the 2nd of February [1942]

How circumstances affect a person! How a common misfortune can bring about unity, closeness, friendship! Yesterday was the thirteenth birthday of Albert Dibovsky, an intelligent Russian boy, well brought up, handsome, likable. He's in the sixth grade, a good student and friend, and also a Pioneer. The whole class decided to arrange a modest banquet for him. They all gathered in the girls' room in the evening and ate supper together. For Albert they obtained a double portion. His Pioneer group leader made a birthday speech, as did one of his friends. After supper they sat around the table for a long time, singing, joking, happily passing the time. Their supervisors, Fanny and B. P., were busy, and the kids were alone all the while. I was at a rehearsal during the first part and arrived following all the speeches. I was moved by their gathering: the whole class was sitting around the table and eating. In the center sat Albert, and on either side the Pioneer leaders. All the kids were dressed up as for a holiday. You felt the warm friendship and intimacy. You don't find it everywhere the way you do among us! Although Albert doesn't know where his parents are, today he didn't feel lonesome or sad. The sincere comradely feelings on his birthday created a loving family for him in the 160-member collective.

A few days ago, Mira Reytsina, a fourteen-year-old Jewish girl in the seventh grade, received a telegram from her mother. Mira is from the eastern part of White Russia, but she came to Bialystok with her parents in 1940. Her mother is a doctor; her father, a Party worker. Mirele is an able, intelligent girl, with thick black hair and dark eyes. She is liked by everyone, even though she's childish and naïve. Her joy after receiving the telegram from her mother was everyone's joy.

Lately a lot of Russian citizens have found their parents. Departing from Druskenik we were 215 children, and now we are down to 160. Fifty-five have already left Karakulino together with their parents, who came to get them. They warmly said good-bye to us, and some of them even write us letters, which makes us feel close to one another. After all, we lived through so much together. Together we escaped from Hitler's planes, survived the fear of bombarding and conflagration, twelve days stuck in a train, starving for several days—without even a drop of water, many days with little to eat, together suffering from cold, filth, even infectious diseases. At first we all longed for home, ached with pain, but then we began to study together, to work together as a community. All of us will retain traces of our life together, many memories for the rest of our lives.

Tuesday the 3rd of February [1942]

Today a mother came to fetch her child—Galya Fateyevna. Galya is thirteen years old and in the sixth grade. Until the war the mother lived in Zabludovo. When the war broke out she took a taxi to Druskenik to get her daughter, but when she arrived there, we had already gone. She became friendly with a military detachment and was evacuated with them. In addition to Galya, she lost three children. After much trouble and a stroke of good luck she found Galya—one child out of four! The poor mother is now bearing up well. Galya's joy is indescribable, as is our own. Some are even crying, though we all share Galya's joy. But we do envy her, too. We remember, after all, that somewhere we also have loving parents, who perhaps are looking for us and certainly suffer and weep.

Today I dreamed about my dear little sister Sorele: I kissed her a lot. It's been so long since I've seen her, the first time in our lives that we've been apart . . . perhaps forever. I remember how she accompanied me to the train, dressed in a brown sweater, how I gave her a cookie through the train window. When the train started to move, I waved to her with a handkerchief and she followed me for a long time with her glances. Sorele, Sorele, you are almost fourteen years old and you've had to suffer so much! Your childhood and early youth were not lived in happy circumstances. The burdens of need and sorrow undoubtedly lie heavy on your weak little shoulders. Darling little sister! You are a little heroine, or else a young martyr, the victim of bloody reactionaries. I don't know, but I hope that you live and flourish and that you help Mama and Papa, along with our brother Moyshl—so that we can reunite and take revenge for your suffering, for the blood of millions of people, for the tears of the sick, the old, the abandoned, and the orphans!!!

Thursday the 5th of February [1942], 11:00 at night

For a long, long time I hadn't experienced the feeling that has now warmed my heart. Suddenly, I forgot the recent experiences, the place where I find myself. I suddenly felt as if I were in my home environment, among my friends.

Today one of the seventh grade students, who sleeps in our dormitory room, turned sixteen. We all decided to arrange a "banquet" for her. We cleaned up the room, set up two long tables covered with tablecloths, and served supper here. Fanny P., our counselor, took care of things for us, getting cookies and candies for us from the administration. We invited two counselors—Fanny P. and B. P. [Berta Pevzner]—Rebecca Izraelevna, the director, Samuil Markovich, Asya, and Tanya. The mood was solemn and intimate. She received many birthday speeches. I prepared the presentations for Beyle and for Lyonya, the class administrator. When I made my own presentation, I spoke about our great friendship, our big new family. But I also mentioned our home, Bialystok, and my mother. At that point my voice trembled with tears. Afterward I couldn't forgive myself, because, after all, I had introduced a mournful tone into the celebration. I tried to inspire some joy and, in the end, succeeded: I began to sing songs from our past and asked everybody to sing along.

Beyle Shepes—our honoree—is a person of good character. After all, she also grew up with a Jewish background, studied in a Yiddish school. She is always the first to join me in a Yiddish song. Today we burst into song together. I was told that I'd become very excited—my cheeks were glowing, my eyes shined brightly and glistened, I gesticulated energetically. My inspired spirit was freed. Right away I felt happy. I was reminded of an evening in our Yiddish *gymnazium*, May Day 1941. Now I realize how good I feel in my own environment. Its traditions and special qualities make me happy. I was raised in it, and it instilled in me a delightful culture that I miss very much.

I notice the same trait in all the kids from the Yiddish schools. The Yiddish songs loosened our tongues and warmed our hearts!

Sunday the 8th of February [1942], 12:30 in the morning

Last night our show had its premiere. We performed for the children in the club. There were a few mistakes—Genya burst out laughing at one point, Shura was late in exiting—but in general it was quite good. Vitaly and the other "actors" from the club—Volodya Ponomarov, a tenth grader, and his friends—made fun of it. I understand why they did: they were sticking up for their friend Vitaly, who very much resented the fact that Zhenya Tchuyev was playing his part and playing it very well! I had the main role and was onstage the entire time. After the performance ended, we all went home filled with many impressions. Rebecca Izraelevna brought cookies and candies for the "actors." For a long, long time we talked about the evening, joking and having fun as we removed the makeup from our faces.

This evening we are performing once again. This time our teachers, all the directors of enterprises, representatives of the Party Committee, of the Komsomol, are invited—the cream of Karakulino society. In addition, we are selling tickets. The money goes to the Defense Fund. We're all full of anxiety about how it will turn out, but we also feel sure that it'll be good.

The only problem is that it's very cold in the clubroom. We perform in light summer dresses and slippers. I've already caught a slight cold. I just hope this performance doesn't cost me what the show in 1936 did: pneumonia, half a year of serious illness. Now I'm very worried about it.

One thing seems funny: after the performance last night, the young people have more respect for me than usual. They call out, "There goes Lida" (that's my name in the play), make room for me at the table, serve me good things, hang around with me. I'm very grateful for the compliment. It proves that I acted well. But I don't want people to look at me differently, as if I were primarily a character in a play.

A problem with the stove: as luck would have it, I'm in charge of the room today and have to clean up all of yesterday's mess, bring in wood, and provide heat. But the wood doesn't want to burn, and I don't have the strength to blow on it. The stove is trying my patience.

Today another one of the girls got a telegram from her mother. It's Clara Baranski. We all congratulated her. Probably all of those from the Eastern Terrritories* will soon have found their parents. That will leave only us—from the Western Territories—alone.

I remember my statement to my brother Mitya in the play: *"Zhizn ochen' slozhna, Mitya, pravda?"* ["Life is very complicated, Mitya, isn't that so?"] And his answer: *"Da, no my yeyo ne boimsya!"* ["Yes, but we do not fear it!"] *"My zhizni ne boimsya!"* ["We are not afraid of life!"] Mitya exclaims. Understandably, I am not afraid of life. I don't know what lies ahead for me—how much hardship, how much unpleasantness—and also how much joy awaits me. But I'm not afraid. I know that everything depends on me alone.

Monday, the 9th of February [1942]

Yesterday at five in the afternoon I went to a fourth grade birthday party, to which I'd been invited. Afterward Helena Pantelemonovna arrived and began applying our makeup for the evening's performance. My makeup worked very well. Everybody liked it a lot, and I was told that I shine when I'm on the stage! Many distinguished guests came to the performance, and a lot of them had bought tickets. We sold tickets worth 380 rubles! The performance was very successful; everyone acted well. We made a very good impression. And I was very pleased! We returned home in a jolly mood, ate some cookies and candy, and rejoiced in the play.

This morning, when we came into the classroom, all the kids were sitting in the back benches, chatting. But as we entered, they interrupted their conversation. We sensed it right away, and realized that they had been speaking about us and the performance. The entire day they said not a single word to us about it. On the other hand, we were highly praised in the tenth grade!

---

* Eastern/Western Territories: the reference is to those territories (eastern) that were part of the USSR prior to 1939, as opposed to the (western) areas annexed in 1939–1940. The latter were quickly overrun by the Germans in 1941, with less chance that family members might have fled in time.

I understood the meaning of the silence when I learned that the same play had been performed last year by several kids in our class: Lida—by Galya Pavlovsky; Vladek—by Vitaly Severukhin; Galya—by Galya Permyakova; Anna—by Manya Neymushina; Sasha—by Anfisa Tyubenkova. But everyone says that our acting was better than theirs! Naturally, they resent that. You can tell there's a certain jealousy, if only to a small degree, because we occupy so prominent a position in school! In fact, we attract the attention of the whole village; even though many of the foreign students from big cities know more Polish than Russian, still we perform in Russian and they respect us for it.

It's possible that we will perform once more on Sunday for the students at school. Probably we'll take on yet another play. I very much want to perform. Overcoming difficulties makes our gray existence more interesting and fulfilling.

After lunch I again went into the empty fourth grade classroom to do my homework. Shura and Liza Zakuta have set themselves up here as well. Liza is fifteen years old and is very ill. She has a constant high temperature [100.4, 101.8° F]. She was in the hospital back in Bialystok, and in Minsk, too, but nothing can be done to help her. The doctors don't know what's wrong. She looks like a corpse—terribly pale, almost green, an emaciated face, sunken cheeks, lifeless eyes. She doesn't go to school, or out in the street, either. She either lies in bed or sits on the bed fully dressed. At first the nurse and doctor treated her badly, arguing that she suffered from hysteria and was physically healthy. But now Fanny P. has been paying a lot of attention to her, and the situation has changed. Lisa is on a special diet: they give her a lot of butter, sugar, sausage, meat, stewed fruit. Her condition has improved a little. She feels that she's being cared for and she's very grateful. She is by nature a very good person, though a bit moody. She has no parents: even back in Bialystok she was being raised in a children's home. I feel sorry for her. What will become of her? She is almost illiterate, seriously ill, cannot survive independently. How will she live? You can't remain in a children's home forever. Her state of health is so hopeless. She is a young child, but hasn't yet known happiness. What sins did she commit? Why is life so unfair to her?

Wednesday the 11th of February [1942]

I am so depressed! Today I had a terrible dream, a night-mare, which left me exhausted and terribly sad. I dreamed that I came back home! I embrace my mother, but, unfortunately, I witness the death of four nursing babies. I see how they bury the four infants, how their mothers weep and tear their hair. One of the mothers is Mrs. Postrigach. Recently I had tutored her daughter Malke, and at that time Mrs. Postrigach was pregnant. The wretched women greet me on my return. Suddenly I see my geography teacher, Olga Petrovna, in a lovely room, along with my friends from the Yiddish elementary school—Mashe Atlas, Fanny Grabowski, Kofler. They're all very sad because we're going to the four little graves with Mrs. Postrigach. My nerves are extremely on edge after such a dream.

Saturday the 14th of February [1942]

Yesterday was an interesting and happy day. After lunch I went with Genya and the other seventh graders from our dormitory to the Kama and learned to ski. I very much enjoyed the beautiful weather in the country. The sky is clear, pure blue, the snow puffy and silvery-white, the air fresh, transparent. It smells of spring, though winter is not yet gone and there will still be frost, unfortunately. Still, the sun warms and a fresh breeze is blowing. I place my feet timidly in the skis and deeply breathe in the refreshing air. It's a pleasure to move along in the dazzling whiteness following the tracks of the skis ahead of me! To see nothing but white snow and a transparent, clear sky! I feel warm, the blood races through my body, my face is ruddy. I don't feel like ever leaving this place. Still, it's starting to get dark. We skied here until supper, then went home to do our homework.

Sunday the 15th of February [1942], 10:30 in the morning

Yesterday I had an interesting talk with one of our seventh graders, Zbiszek Mak. Zbiszek is over fifteen years old, Polish by nationality. He is quite short, with blond hair and a typical Polish appearance. And, in fact, he is a Polish patriot. Maybe formerly he was even an anti-Semite. He is very capable and intelligent, although still quite childish. He also took part in the play that we performed, taking the role of my brother, Mitya. He played the part very well. It came as a surprise, because he is usually cool and indifferent toward the projects that we undertake. He hardly ever does his homework and gets by only on his ability. He plans to transfer to a manual-training school in order to learn a trade. I was amazed that he didn't want study, because at home he would surely be a student. He would certainly grow up to be an intelligent person pursuing intellectual work. I decided to have a talk with him, because I understood the reason for his attitude: he feels alienated among us, out of his element. Doesn't he realize that in our international community—among Jews, Russians, Byelorussians, and Poles—nobody makes distinctions between one or the other? Everyone is rewarded according to his work and punished according to his sins. For one so lacking in awareness, this really must be something new. His closest friends are the well-known quintet of Polish boys who are not students, but instead help out in the kitchen. When Zbiszek found out that they planned to send them to vocational school, he decided not to be separated from them, but to go along. This is how he's ruining his career. I explained to him that it's a poor choice, that he would be better off continuing his studies. Zbiszek spoke to me openly and intimately, and he thanked me warmly for our conversation. I should like to maintain my friendship with him. I want him to grow up to be a good, cultivated person.

Today at noon we performed again for the students at school. Again we put on makeup, and afterward I remained with Helena Pantelemonovna. She started to tell me the story of her life: she is a very talented woman—an actress, an artist—but she couldn't complete her studies because of financial circumstances. She began to study acting in Stanislavski's studio in Moscow, but she didn't have the opportunity to finish. Now she teaches drawing to the fourth grade. Her husband is at the front, and she has remained here with her little boy. She said to me sadly, "My life is broken forever!" She also told me that she was in a children's home as a child and suffered a great deal. Life raised her very high because she stood out with her talent, but now she has fallen low because her talent is being wasted.

I like her very much, and I'd love to spend time talking with her, but, to our mutual regret, I had to interrupt the conversation, because the performance was starting. I'll try to talk to her later. Perhaps she can advise me; she is such a kind, cultivated, talented, sincere woman!

Monday February 16th [1942]

Yesterday I did something ugly: I found my friend's diary on the table, so I started to read it. My curiosity drove me to a despicable act. It's the same thing as climbing into someone's heart with dirty boots! Why did I do it?

The diary is written in Polish. The period of our stay in Sarapul is briefly described. Nothing of interest in general is to be found here. She described her relationship with the director. I was astonished by how she defines it: she is his lover! Oh, she's nothing more than the object of his passions. Did I really fail to notice before? After all, she lay in his arms every night. Does this nineteen-year-old girl love him? She doesn't write about that at all. It seems to me, no, she is just too weak to resist him. She's happy when he brings her additional rations: butter, sugar, bread. Does she believe in his love? It seems to me that she doesn't! After all, she knows that in Sarapul young women would often visit him. She knows that last year, in Druskenik, he flirted with the Pioneer leader and this year with Dr. Berger. Oh, she is so lightheaded.

Yesterday I accidentally broke the right lens of my eyeglasses. I am very worried, though for the time being the lens is still in place and I can use it. Anna Mikhailovna, Volodya's aunt, told me yesterday that she knows the whereabouts of my old glasses, the ones I've almost forgotten about. She couldn't tell me yet, because she isn't sure that the two individuals whom she has to ask about it will give her the information. Maybe the day after tomorrow she'll tell me. I think that this has to do with Volodya and Vitaly. Is it perhaps their doing? I remember that on the very evening that the glasses disappeared they came to my bed (I was sick). Perhaps the glasses were lying on the chair near the bed. Why did they take them away? Maybe it was a joke, or maybe they intended to cause me real unhappiness. It will be interesting if Anna Mikhailovna can let me know tomorrow. What must I do in order to get my glasses back? What if they deny everything, or break the glasses—what will I do?

Tuesday the 17th of February [1942]

Yesterday at the drama circle we read a new play, *Platon Krechet.*[*] We began assigning the parts. Everyone said that I should play Lida, the main character. But Shura cried out that she wanted to play the main part. That's because she suffers from megalomania. Her mother, Fanny P., asked Helena Pantelemonovna to let me play the mother, and have her daughter play Lida. I've already played the role of Lida and everyone complimented me, so why switch parts? Helena Pantelemonovna told me that she wants me to play the mother because it's a very difficult role, and she doesn't know who else could play it. She also convinced me that although it's not the main part, still it's a serious and sympathetic role, Platon's mother. The mother of a hero of science, compared to Lida, who is young and pretty, but not serious. So I'll be playing two parts: one evening, Lida, and the second evening, the mother, Maria Tarasovna.

Zbiszek advises me to do it; he also wants me to play the mother. He and I have a good relationship. Formerly an anti-Semite, now a clever, kind, and capable fifteen-year-old youth, he considers me a close friend!

[*] By the Soviet Ukrainian dramatist Aleksandr Korneichuk (1906–1972).

Wednesday the 18th of February [1942], 3:30 in the afternoon

Lately there has been a lot of heartache. Today, for example, Genya got a letter from a friend who was evacuated to Tashkent, saying that she was unemployed, homeless, lonely, and very hungry. Genya has been crying the whole day. And though I'm not crying, it still reminds me of the situation in the country and of everyone's fate. We are all hungry, after eight months of war and the first wartime winter. What will happen in the summer? Who will plant and produce the food? There is a campaign going on now among the young people in school: the upper grades are signing up for courses as tractor drivers—in my class as well. But I'm not enrolled, because when classes started I didn't have my glasses and couldn't properly see the diagrams of the fields. But come summer I'll have to work all the same in the fields used by our food service. It is too late to start the [tractor] course now, since the class is already far along.

Our children's home is paradise compared to the rest of the country. At a time when hardworking people are starving, we have food, though it is often not enough. But in comparison, we are better off, though it's not like it was in our homes before the war. We now have a clean bed and a warm room, and we are studying! So we need to work, too! Enough self-contemplation! I even want to stop my diary writing for a while, so that I can learn to behave differently, better!

Monday the 2nd of March [1942]

I had decided not to keep my diary anymore, so I haven't written for two weeks. Now I can't resist! The director has been attacking me again. I've been taking less care of business at the children's council. Why? Because the work no longer satisfies me. I'm more involved with my education! As a result, lately he's forbidden me to play my two parts, as if that were the cause of my poor work! He is even trying to exclude me altogether from the drama circle. But Rebecca Izraelevna defends me and assures me that I'll continue to perform in the play.

Sunday the 8th of March [1942], 12:00 noon

Lately I've started to read intensively and also have taken up community work. I led a session of the housekeeping committee, and Friday I was on duty myself in the kitchen all day. And I prepared a talk that I gave yesterday to the older children and the entire staff. Many people congratulated me on my talk. They were all glad that I've begun to work again. Yesterday I felt bad, and in the middle of the evening, when everybody was so happy, I went off by myself to our room, unmade the bed, and went to sleep. Today I still feel bad.

My glasses are still broken, so I can't use them. I have a slight hope that I'll get new, good glasses. I want the director to take me with him to Izhevsk so that I can visit a doctor who will fit me with new glasses. But he doesn't want to take me along. He never stops making sarcastic remarks, explaining that his brother Boris put on glasses because it was very modern, and hints that it's the same thing with me! It pains me that my vision is so poor—from the distance of one meter I can't see someone's eyes, just dark holes. In the evening I don't recognize objects, even up close. With my new glasses I could hardly see the actors onstage from the front row at the club! I now feel my misfortune so much more strongly than before, when I wore the glasses that so mysteriously disappeared. I'm suffering and nobody wants to understand me. The director has tried to get hold of my talk in order to minimize its worth. He made a fuss at the presidium, in order to make trouble for me. He picked on the fact that I sent him a greeting (we sent greetings and gifts in the form of letters to the whole staff).

All the counselors, Rebecca Izraelevna, and all the older kids in the seventh grade are indignant that he's been harassing me. I am not indifferent either. I believe that I haven't deserved this treatment. I am in a bad mood. I haven't been happy for a long time, do not laugh, do not sing. I don't even care about my appearance. First of all, I don't have a single piece of dressy clothing, no slippers; I comb my hair any old way. Lately I have noticed that Volodya Ponomarev, a student in the tenth grade, is paying attention to me. He recently said that of all the girls at the children's home, he likes Lena, in the ninth grade, the best. That's what my girlfriends in the ninth grade told me. I am very surprised.

Lena, March 1942

Monday the 16th of March [1942]

Lately I have been thinking about my future. What will I be doing during the second school year? Genya and Tanya are thinking about an institute in Sverdlovsk [Ekaterinburg] or Molotov [Perm]. Next summer they intend to send applications and requests for admission there. When they leave, I will remain all alone, without any close friends—all alone in a collective of grown-up children, sixteen- and seventeen-year-olds. It would be nice if I didn't have to part with those who are closest to me, if I could go with them to the institute. But to do that you must have passed your tenth grade examinations, and I am only in the ninth grade.

Lately we hear on the radio that there's no news from the front. What does it mean? Maybe the enemy is once again mobilizing for a fierce attack? Who knows?

Recently I was photographed, and I was given the photo. My features are so out of proportion: small nearsighted eyes, underneath which thin little wrinkles and dark hollows have appeared, and a face that is partly covered with red pimples.

Tuesday the 17th of March [1942], 10:00 in the evening

Today I did not go to school, because I had to prepare a lecture about the Eighteenth of March.* I was ordered to do it, because everybody liked my first talk. So tomorrow I'll give the lecture. I've been going around for more than ten days without glasses, because mine are broken. It's very difficult now. The first few days were especially hard to endure, but now I've gotten used to it a bit.

I'll soon be going to Izhevsk to see a doctor, and perhaps there I can get glasses. I've been waiting for a while for a horse and wagon to take me there. I believe that in a few days there will be one.

Thursday the 26th of March [1942]

I've returned from my long trip. For an entire week I was away, and I did not go to school. Unexpectedly, on Wednesday the eighteenth, right after my report, I left for Izhevsk, where I stayed for two days, and from where I returned yesterday afternoon. The trip was very unsuccessful, because my face was frostbitten, especially the right side, which became very swollen and painful. On my right cheek I have a boil! The most important thing: the eye doctor in Izhevsk prescribed glasses, but I couldn't get them in Izhevsk. I was desperate: what will I do? How will I be able to study? Now I'm beginning to make some peace with my fate, because I'm hopeful about the director's promise that he'll get the glasses in Sarapul from a private optician. The trip showed me a lot of things, and now I have no regrets that I went. I became a bit acquainted with the lives of the peasants with whom I happened to stay during the trip. They are all very poor, and live in dark, crowded huts. Barefoot children dressed in rags sit on the oven. They have little to eat. It's completely different from the kolkhoz people I read about in books or saw on the stage, or on the screen! In the cities the situation is also difficult. Speculation has increased

---

* The reference presumably is to the Paris Commune, which was proclaimed on March 18, 1871.

tremendously, and many foods are hard to get altogether. People are dying of hunger! So in our children's home in Karakulino we live under the best conditions.

Now I do not regret my trip, despite the fact than it ended without any luck.

Friday the 27th of March [1942]

I didn't sleep the whole night. I was thinking, thinking . . . about what?

Today or tomorrow we are performing *Platon Krechet* in the club. I play the mother, and Shura plays Lida, the leading role, which I had played previously.

Everyone can see that Shura doesn't feel what she says, that she's simply learned the sounds by rote. But she cannot convey the facial expressions and gestures during rehearsals. Various oddities that make the audience laugh and Helena Pantelemonovna and Rebecca Izraelevna nervous. They all say that Shura is very dull. I had earlier wanted to play Lida, but she also wanted to, and her mother, Fanny P., asked that she be given the part. Now it is of no importance to me; in any case, I couldn't play Lida now because my cheek is still bandaged after five days. I won't put on any makeup, just wear a gray wig. Maybe I'll cover up the bandage with my kerchief, but will it work? Nobody has said anything and I don't know what will happen. But it's a fact that my acting now is a secondary matter.

Sunday the 12th of April [1942], 11:00 in the evening

Today we had an evening devoted to the works of Nekrasov.[*] I was responsible, and the evening went very well. The director said some nice words about me. My cheek is getting a little better, but it's still not normal. Despite the fact that this has been going on for three weeks now, the doctor won't permit me to remove

---

[*] Nikolai Alekseyevich Nekrasov (1821–1877), Russian poet and publisher.

the bandage. I can't even hope that it will be removed by the first of May. I probably won't get my glasses either. These two modest, but very important, wishes of mine will apparently not be fulfilled.

Several days ago in the library I accidentally found Yitzkhok Leybush Peretz's[*] short stories in Russian translation: "*Der Meshulekh*," [The Messenger], "*Bontshe Shvayg*" [Bontshe the Silent] "*Di Levone Dertseylt*" [The Moon Recounts] and so on. I was overjoyed! I read it aloud for the girls in the dormitory, and explained it to them. I felt so proud. If not for my conscience, I would simply have filched the book! The work is so familiar, so close to me. And despite the fact that the book is in Russian, it still has great value because it's a good translation. I feel it in Yiddish and I even tried to read it directly in Yiddish. It turned out pretty well. Now where can I find a Yiddish book? I so long for the spiritual nourishment!

Tuesday the 14th of April [1942]

They did not bring me my glasses! It seems that I won't have them so soon. Maybe when the war is over, maybe even later. What a horror! I can see absolutely nothing on the blackboard! This hinders me a lot, especially in physics and mathematics.

Rebecca Izraelevna shows a lot of interest in me. She's even told me that when the war ends she'll take me home with her and arrange for me to study so that I can take care of myself. She expressed admiration for my knowledge of the Yiddish language when she heard several excerpts from my diary. She was delighted with my writing ability. I told her that I'd tried to write at home— and not without success. She told me that Professor Nusinov[†] was her personal friend; and that if I were in Moscow, she would introduce me to him as well as to the circle of Yiddish writers and cultural activists. What a magnificent dream!

[*] I. L. Peretz (1852–1915): with Mendele Mocher Sforim and Sholem Aleichem, one of the masters of classic Yiddish literature; often considered the first modern Yiddish writer.

[†] Isaac Nusinov (1889–1952), Soviet Yiddish literary critic and historian. He was arrested in 1948 and executed in August 1952, along with many other Soviet Yiddish writers.

Leise zieht durch mein Gemüt
Liebliches Geläute.
Klinge, kleines Frühlingslied
Kling hinaus ins Weite!

Kling hinaus bis an das Haus
Wo die Blumen sprießen.
Wenn du eine Rose schaust.
Sag' ich laß sie grüßen!
                              —Heine

[Gently moving through my soul
A delightful ringing.
Ring, little song of spring
Right out into the world!

Ring out to the house
Where flowers sprout.
If you see a rose there
Tell her that I greet her!]

Monday the 20th of April [1942]

What a terrible time we are living through! Exiled in a remote village in Udmurtia, more than 2,000 kilometers from the front and the war zone, having a warm, bright nook, with enough to eat, I often forget what a situation the country finds itself in. Only distant echoes reach my ear from time to time and make my blood run cold. People who have come from the Leningrad region tell me that cannibalism has become widespread! Mothers kill and eat their own children! Horrors!!!

"V mire yest tsar, etot tsar besposhchadien, golod nazvanie yemu!" —Nekrasov, "Zheleznaya Doroga"[*]

---

[*] In the world there is a tsar, this tsar is merciless, hunger is his name! (Nekrasov, "The Railway")

Hunger! Constant cramps in an empty stomach, swollen bodies, gloomy faces, bags of bones covered by thin membranes, toothless mouths, powerless hands. Shadow-people, living corpses with extinguished eyes. Oh, cruel tsar—hunger! In your bony fingers the country wheezes and suffocates. The people breathe in your icy breath. In most of the cities, typhus and other epidemics rage, sisters by blood of the tsar, hunger.

The countryside is getting ready for spring planting. With all its strength the nation wrestles with the cruel ruler. Soon the spring planting will begin, and everybody is being mobilized. Soon spring will come, together with a breakthrough on the front. A strong attack by the enemy is expected, a final battle that will decide the outcome of the war. In the country there is a total mobilization. They are even mobilizing invalids who were previously discharged; they're mobilizing old people, in order to use their skills in the hinterland. Both sides are getting ready. The time is coming when the radio will stop repeating, "No news on the Western front!" The news will come quickly, but what kind? What will it bring to the country and its people? Will it bring back peace? Reconstruction of the country? Quiet happiness?

Tuesday the 28th of April [1942]

Director Pevzner's sister has managed to be evacuated from Leningrad. A few days ago, he left to meet her, and then he brought her here. What a horror! She can hardly move. As a result of long starvation, her hands and feet have become paralyzed. She tells how people fell down in the street from hunger. They even stopped having funerals; the corpses were taken from the streets and buried in a common grave. If anyone wants more bread than the 400 grams that are rationed, he has to pay 400 rubles for a kilogram of bread! One kilogram of butter costs 1,500 rubles!* The city is under a constant siege; the enemy is 30 kilometers away in Pushkinskoe Selo [the tsar's village near Leningrad].

*For purposes of comparison, 1,500 rubles would have been six months' salary for a working-class employee.

She brought the terrible news that Pevzner's father and Berta P.'s husband have died. All this news has put everyone in a dreadful mood. After all, these consequences of the war were unknown to us.

Now it is spring: warm, sunny days. Already we feel more cheerful. A few days ago I wrote a sketch about spring in Russian:

Spring!

Suddenly, without notice, the frosts have vanished, rain has fallen and moistened the earth. Fresh, damp winds stroll across the land and awaken the weather from its long winter sleep. The weather scatters slowly and powerfully. Every day it brings forth joy and life; every day there is something new and fresh.

On one such day I felt spring for the first time. It flowed into my blood, and I went out for a stroll. I wandered around the nearby hills, in the newly drenched wet earth; I breathed in the fresh, clean air, contemplated the blue that enveloped me and caught the gold poured out by the sun. Spring is so beautiful! I thought, and my heart beat more vigorously in my breast. My feet carried me further. I wanted to go still further into the unknown. I was overwhelmed by this display of the power of weather. My gaze fell on a splendid valley, friendly little white houses surrounded by gardens, a small group of majestic trees. How calm and festive it is here! The changeable moist air abounds with the diverse abundance of life. Streams pour over my feet. They have made their way between the earth and the rocks, rushing merrily and playfully washing the ground under my feet! From all directions the waters converge, gushing into streams and, with uncommon force, descending with a roar that bespeaks their power. I stood alone in the water in my drenched coat. The wind played with everything beneath it, tearing the hat from my head as if we were obliged to greet the advancing weather: "Life is good!"

I remembered the war. A few hundred kilometers away from us spring is in bloom, the earth awakens, but over there the spring rivulets are sprinkled with warm human blood. Over there the German bandits are killing Soviet citizens, murdering women and children. The shoes of the barbarians trample our holy earth in this pleasant springtime. At this thought my heart shuddered, filled with burning hatred. I observed the streams join and surge, and I thought to myself: That is how our people gathers together all its strength, prepares to attack the enemy. That is how the waters of the family's true sons flow to the front.

The water surrounded me and receded. At the very top there lay a stone. The water had washed over it and finally flung it below, where it continued to drift. "May that be the fate of the enemy!" They will be killed, annihilated. The Soviet people will defend its soil, its spring, its life. We will kill the enemy and return to peace.

Apparently the streams sensed my thoughts and sped ever more merrily on their way.

Monday the 4th of May [1942]

Why do I now write less often in my diary? Because my mood has radically changed. My melancholy has disappeared along with the cold weather. My frame of mind has brightened. Perhaps it's because I began to fight back against the emptiness and lethargy that dominated me earlier. Now I am more interested in living life than in writing about it in a diary. Still I want to preserve on paper not only my heartache, but also my love of life.

The twenty-eighth of April was Shloyme Furman's birthday. The twenty-eighth of April, 1939, he gave me his photo and a little copper heart with his monogram. But it remained at home in a drawer. That's why I don't have it with me now. Shloyme has now turned eighteen. What's happening to him now at home? Is he alive? Is he well?

A few days ago it was May Day. A year ago I revealed my feelings to Zavl Rubinovich. We used to meet every day, take walks together, talk, but later, while we were traveling to Druskenik, we suddenly broke up. It ended so sadly, so seriously. Is Zavl still alive? Who knows? The fate of all my friends is grievous. Dear friends, I wish I could help you, but what can I do? Unfortunately I am helpless!

Thursday the 7th of May [1942]

Lately I want to achieve something, to grow spiritually, to learn a great deal. I dream of being in a big city, in a cultural milieu, where I can study. I contemplate choosing the Faculty of Literature and studying foreign languages. Sometimes I think that perhaps I will be able to write. Who knows? I want to leave the rank of the gray, average bourgeois person, I want to ascend to the heights, to the sun! Where do the beauty and interest of life lie? Is it only in the enjoyment of the passions, in living through different experiences? In my view, no! Life's interest lies in creativity! Every person who lives not only to eat, sleep, and dress well must bring to society something new, creative, in order to enrich humanity, to leave a trace behind even when one's ashes disappear into eternity. In order to create, you have to study for a long time, learn from the geniuses of the past, embrace thinking and creative spirit for the sake of your grandchildren. Lately this thought has come to me. When I look at those around me, it seems that most of them have no such goal.

Sunday the 17th of May [1942]

Summer arrived suddenly, as suddenly as spring. A week ago, everyone was still wearing winter coats, shoes and stockings. Today was already as hot as a day in July back home. All the kids threw off their warm clothes, put on light dresses, and headed for the outdoors! Our courtyard is very big, overgrown with trees, which form several avenues! On the green lawn you find children's bodies and green, red, white, and blue dresses. You hear shouts, laughter, and singing. The sun is very hot today, and people are already getting sunburned. I sat in the sun in order to tan the big spot on my right cheek, which is a remnant of my wound. It was only yesterday that I removed the bandage that I'd worn for ten weeks. In three days exams begin, but I haven't yet begun to prepare for them because I've been warming myself in the sun and going for walks. I am enraptured by nature; there are places here that enchant and intoxicate you. Yesterday evening we climbed uphill and down, jumped over a narrow stream, leaped over brooks. A panorama of hills, all newly green, came into view. A bit farther was the Kama, which broadly overflowed its banks, even inundating the nearby villages. On the Kama there were small rowboats and sailboats. Nestled between the hills is a small valley, with some houses surrounded by newly plowed gardens and a lake bordered by a few young trees. All around is absolute stillness: no breeze, no trembling blade of grass. Overlooking this scene, it seems that the sky is a transparent blue and the sun is rolling to the west. Many emotions fill my heart. The mood is cheerful and relaxed. Later, we climb down from the summit and gather at the river's edge. Now evening descends on the water, first on the shore, which grows darker, light purple. Then it gradually comes closer until it swallows up the sky and water. There is even a little boat, which approaches, lies in wait, and beckons to us.

The work at the children's home is slowly being transformed. We are going over to agriculture. For two weeks already I've been working in our garden: plowing and planting carrots, onions, and beets. I actually got a lot of pleasure from the work. Now I begin to understand Tolstoy and his theory of standing closer to nature and to the earth: I feel that I'll soon grow to love the earth, which, thanks to my sweat and labor, brings me fruit and nourishes me. Altogether, I have the impression that I'm living in peacetime in a dacha, a country house. Here, everything is so beautiful, festive, that it has a good effect on my nerves. My winter moods have disappeared. I am full of life—and joy in my work!

May has come to us once more
With its splendid magic powers
And awakened once again
All the grass and all the flowers[*]

Friday the 22nd of May [1942]

Today is the second day of final examinations. Yesterday we took the written examination in Russian, a composition. I wrote a critique of Bazarov, the hero of Turgenev's work, *Fathers and Sons*. I compared him to Lopukhov and Kirsanov in Chernyshevsky's *What Is to Be Done*.[†] I've already learned that I did well and got a grade of "excellent"! Today at nine o'clock we have the written exam in algebra—after that, the oral examination in geometry. On the twenty-sixth of May the school year ends, and then we'll be out again in the field and garden.

My plans to attend college have burst like a soap bubble. The *Narkom* [minister of education] was here recently, and we spoke with him. From the ninth grade I can be accepted only at an institute that trains teachers for the fifth to seventh grades. That does not interest me. This summer I need to prepare the coursework for the tenth grade and pass with a grade of "excellent" at our school. I've decided to finish the tenth grade here. And after that? Who knows? Maybe the war will end and I will have better prospects?

Saturday the 23rd of May [1942]

Life is much stronger than the individual, who's nothing but a tiny grain of sand on the ocean's shore. Life teaches us to uproot the past in order to be ready for the present and struggle for

[*] Sung in the prewar Yiddish schools in Poland.

[†] Nikolai Chernyshevsky (1828–1889), Russian Socialist publisher and writer. His novel *What Is to Be Done* (1863) was written in reaction to the portrayal of young radicals in Turgenev's celebrated *Fathers and Sons* (1862).

the future. No matter how much we try to keep images of the past in our memory, we must still create new impressions that displace the earlier ones.

The twentieth of May, three days ago, was my brother Moyshele's sixteenth birthday! And I—how cruel—reminded myself about it only late that evening. What a disgrace! Moyshele, may you live a long time! Live for yourself and for our future!

My dear family! Mama and Papa always hoped for a good future for the children. Sadly, I am very far from you. I'm absorbed only in myself, and unfortunately cannot help you. Just as in the past, must I suffer from this longing for an entire winter, again fall into a deep depression, and do nothing more even for myself? No! Stubbornly I must build my own life so that when we meet again, I'll be able to help you, to liberate you.

Life is ruthless, but I must make peace with it because I'm young and I want to live. In order to study, I have to be selfish; for in my struggle for existence I must be strong.

Monday the 25th of May [1942]

I just came back from my last exam, geometry. I finally completed the ninth grade. Now I face a three-month break in my studies and work in the fields. I'll be working as a teacher's assistant, as a volunteer. But I also want to accomplish a lot during that time. I must do a lot of reading, review Russian literature from the fifth to seventh grades, material that I hadn't studied before. And I have to again review Russian grammar, although I wrote the exam without a single mistake, receiving a grade of "Excellent." However, at times I feel like writing something. If I have the time and the right mood, I'll start writing a story.

Thursday the 28th of May [1942], 1:00 in the afternoon

I have been replacing Fanny Pavlovna for the first half of the day. That doesn't take a lot of work. After two in the afternoon I am free and I can do what I like. These days I walk, I read, I rest. Yesterday I was on duty until two in the morning at the fire in which we burned the old leaves from last year. Volodya Leonov sat with me. He brought sugar, then potatoes, which we baked and ate. Volodya told some stories, made jokes. . . . It was fun.

For some time I've become more friendly with Helena Pantelemonovna, our stage manager. It began with a minor disagreement. I said that *I Burn Paris* was by Bruno Jasienski, and she said it was by Barbusse.[*] She proposed a bet "with an American woman,"[†] and I won! I asked her three questions: (1) What does she think of me? (2) What roles did she play at the time that she was acting and studying in Stanislavski's studio? (3) What are her thoughts on love and friendship? I also expressed three wishes: (1) to have her photograph; (2) to have one of her artistic paintings or drawings. (3) to have her tell me about her life.

Several weeks have passed since that conversation. I meet her very often, I come to her home. She still has not answered all my questions and requests, but we've had very interesting discussions. She has already shown me some of her early works, when she was a student in art school. In her person I have encountered an intelligent, talented woman! I can learn a lot from her. She is gifted in

---

[*] Bruno Jasienski, born Wiktor Bruno Zysman (1901–1939), Polish-Russian leftist writer. His *Pale Paryz* (1928) was translated into Yiddish as *Kh'bren Pariz* (I Burn Paris). He emigrated to the USSR in 1929, was arrested in 1937, and died on his way to a concentration camp in Siberia.

Henri Barbusse (1873–1935), French writer, was made famous by his World War I novel *Le Feu* (Under Fire). He later became a fervent Communist and died during a visit to Moscow in 1935.

[†] A form of betting whereby the loser has to answer personal questions truthfully.

many ways, has great artistic ability, is accomplished in drawing and painting. Because of her financial situation, unfortunately, she was unable to develop her talent. Now she sits out here in Karakulino and is a teacher. She speaks of herself as a worn-out, faded person, though she's only thirty years old! Pointing to a photograph from her childhood, she said: "This little girl promised much, but delivered nothing!"

I like her very much, have found in her a close friend, a deep person, who understands me and wants to help me make sense of the complicated circumstances of my life.

Sunday the 31st of May [1942]

Last night, unknown to the administration, I slept in the garden of the courtyard. Genya and I found hammocks, snatched some pillows, and slept quite peacefully. Peacefully, except for the mosquitoes biting us. At three in the morning we went back to our room, quickly, so that nobody would see us from outside. At four in the morning, along with girls from the seventh grade, we went off to the fields to plant potatoes. We worked there until eight thirty. We work a lot in the fields now. Every morning four to five hours, in the afternoon three to four hours. In between, there are lunch and meetings. I have little time left for reading. All day long I am busy with farming and administrative work.

Thursday the 4th of June [1942]

The days go by quickly and are filled with impressions. One evening several days ago, I went without the administration's permission to the Kama, the river, and rowed until two in the morning. I enjoyed it so much. Yesterday we spent the whole morning dragging sacks of oats onto the dock. Later in the day, at school, we had an evening devoted to the end of the school year and Honors awards. I also got an award. Later, Vitaly taught me how to ride a bicycle. He was a good teacher and I managed to ride the bicycle very well!

Thursday the 11th of June [1942]

On my right cheek there is a huge dark spot—permanent evidence of my winter disaster. I'm fortunate that in the entire children's home there is not a single mirror, and I don't know what I look like. For that reason I forget my ugliness. Yesterday I got hold of a little mirror by accident and took a look at myself. Why must I be so ugly? I don't ascribe any importance to the external appearance of a person, myself included. But why can't I be tolerable? There are those (and I among them) who give the impression of being cold, severe. Am I truly that way in reality?

The spot is not getting better or getting any lighter. I want to go to the doctor in Sarapul. Maybe he can do something to help?

Wednesday the 17th of June [1942]

In connection with a visit to the children's home by a commission of the Narkompros, work at the home was reorganized for the whole summer. I managed to distribute the committee work and organize groups of kids into work teams, depending on what their health allowed. All of us cleaned our space ourselves: the rooms, kitchen, corridor. We washed dishes and served the meals.

We also organized brigades whose job it is to wash the kids and their laundry, and to iron the underwear and clothing. Brigades harvest the vegetables from our garden, carry in water and even bread.

All the older kids worked at these chores. The younger ones also participated in brigades, under the supervision of their counselors. Every evening at six o'clock—just before supper—all those on duty and all the brigade leaders report to the member of the children's council on duty about the work they have performed, and also to me, since I am the chair of the children's council. Then the tasks for the next day are assigned. Such organization makes it possible to do the work accurately and to supervise how the work is being carried out.

Genya and Tanya are no longer at the home. Genya left for Saratov, and Tanya for Izhevsk. Officially, it was in order to bring some children to their parents, or to the doctor. In reality, in order to get information about the requirements for higher education, since they have already completed the tenth grade.

The situation at the front is not good, despite the agreement with England and America to create a second front.[*] The economic situation in the hinterland is likewise no better. How will it be in the future? Who knows . . .

Monday the 22nd of June [1942]

Today it is one year since the war started. A year ago, looking out the window of the train that was speeding from Druskenik to Bialystok (and never got there!), I was horrified by the red sky of burning Grodno, by the crash of incendiary bombs and the roar of German bombers. At that time I hadn't yet fully appreciated or understood what the war would bring us. I believed that we would make it home! Now I am farther from the frontline and I can't actually see the horror of war. But we have already been informed that there are 700,000 people missing whose whereabouts are unknown, and millions of dead and wounded! People on crutches, without hands, without chins, with feet frozen off, crippled faces and bodies . . . women without husbands, mothers without sons. Every day, children mourn fathers and brothers who have perished. In our class two girls have lost their fathers, and Vitaly his nineteen-year-old brother. There are many miserable orphans in the Soviet Union and throughout the world. No newspaper writes about it, no songs are sung about it, because the resolve to fight has to be strengthened and the idea of freedom developed. But the situation is heartbreaking; all is quiet on the Western front. All hopes for the spring and summer have evaporated. Stalin said in his speech that the war must be ended in 1942. How can that happen?

Now there is terrible starvation in the land, and soon it will be even worse. The country is mobilizing its last resources, its last labor reserves; and if the war lasts much longer we will lose more in

[*] In Western Europe.

the economic sphere than in the political. Even in the countryside, the food situation is difficult: a *pud* [equal to about 36 pounds] of potatoes costs 180 rubles in Karakulino. Flour is worth its weight in gold! There isn't even any kasha, no vegetables, soap, kerosene, matches, salt, not to mention even a minimum amount of knitwear! A needle costs 15 rubles here. In Sarapul, Izhevsk, Kazan, and Saratov, things are much worse. Work in the factories and enterprises is slacker than before, because, after all, it's wartime! What will happen later?

Saturday the 27th of June [1942]

The days are filled with work now: on duty in the kitchen, in the dining room, in the main building; work in the garden, work with the brigades. From time to time I feel anxious: I had made such big, fine plans for the summer. I had decided to read a lot, but unfortunately I'm unable to do it. I wanted to complete the literature program of the eighth and tenth grade Russian classes, and in addition to become acquainted with European literature. I would need to read at least two hours a day—without fail! Sad to say, I cannot do it.

Saturday the 4th of July [1942]

In the course of several days my mood, my psychology, and my future have changed. I've pulled myself out of the everyday grayness, the narrow hardships of working in a children's home, and have reinstated my earlier program.

Three days ago Genya returned from Saratov. She brought back with her a loftier mood, the atmosphere of the city. She told me about the events of her trip, about Saratov, its cultural life, the institute where she submitted her application. Genya has registered in the Faculty of Philology of the evacuated Moscow University and made friends with a lot of students. She also told me that she spoke to the director about me, and he advised her that I should prepare the tenth grade course work during vacation, and take exams at school here in order to obtain a certificate that I have completed tenth grade. When Genya told me this, I wanted to do it, I agreed to it—yes! I am crazy with joy: at night I crawled into her bed and kissed her! Now I wonder how I could be overcome with such madness. I imagined that I was already in Saratov, in the city, in a cultural environment! My constant dream of leaving this remote backwater, Karakulino, is not so far off! The kids in the room stared at me in amazement. I gave no thought to the question of how realistic my plan is, or about the heavy burden I have placed on my shoulders.

That same evening I spoke with the director of the children's home, asking him to free me from communal work. He granted my request. In the morning, I went to school and spoke with the director, Mikhail Ivanovich, and he agreed to it as well. This is how it begins: physics, algebra, geometry, trigonometry, chemistry, and German. In August: literature and history!

I believe that I can succeed, although it's a heavy load. In summer, to sit all the time and study, to have no time to go for a walk, not even to rest. I know that studying at a university also involves great hardships: you have to take care of your material needs, fill in the gaps, which in my case are numerous! But even so, I believe that I'll attain my goal.

Genya is now working in a kindergarten at a collective farm in order to earn bread money for the winter.

Today I heard on the radio that we have evacuated Sevastopol. The port city was heroically defended for more than half a year, and, finally, it has fallen. This is a repetition of last summer. I am overcome with worry: what's going to happen?

Friday the 10th of July [1942]

I have been studying for eight days now. I've been through the entire physics course and I've begun to study literature. When I asked for three more days to prepare for the exam, Aleksey Sergeyevich told me that he had already entered a grade! Then he immediately left for Sarapul. A pity! I didn't want to take advantage of his "generosity"; I wanted to take the exam honestly and conscientiously. I still have a lot of homework and exams to prepare. By the end of the month: literature, chemistry, German. In August: algebra, geometry, trigonometry, history. Meanwhile, I am immersed in Gorky's writings. Even the tenth time I read his works they have an extraordinary effect on me, and I very much regret that my time is so limited that I can't go into them more deeply.

Sunday the 12th of July [1942]

Temptation, temptation, where will you lead me?

You'd think, when you have little time to prepare for exams that you'd know what needs to be done. Perhaps work without letup? Get up at four in the morning? Study till midnight? No! I chose a better way: I spent a whole day on the other bank of the Kama. I picked flowers and red berries, bathed! I didn't think about studying at all. Someone might call it a case of lightheadedness! But the weather is so beautiful, the sky light blue, the Kama cool. The boat rocks lightly in the water and I see a lovely spot, then golden stalks, a young walnut grove, bunches of flowers, and an abundance of juicy, red berries. Summer—the loveliest time of the year! A pity that I can't often spend time in such a palace of nature. It's so pleasant to be here now! Harebrained hothead, weak-willed creature, enough carrying on about the weather! You're satisfied, it's enough. Time to get busy with exams! I become serious and begin to study. I get going in my philosophic thinking. After all, I have to prepare literature, mathematics, chemistry, history!

My youth, with its summer, its green woods, its cool river, and red berries—was all lightheadedness and disarray.

Thursday the 16th of July [1942]

Lately the military situation has become significantly worse: battles at the gates of Voronezh. Every day the enemy captures a few cities, and Saratov* is only 400 km from Voronezh! So how can I go there to study?

Saturday the 18th of July [1942]

The military situation has gotten much worse. Every day the radio brings news that surpasses previous reports in its horror. The enemy is driving us back on all fronts. Battles around Voronezh, new attacks on Moscow and Leningrad! In the meantime we are losing the war. There's not a trace of a second front, about which so much has been said—it's just a delusion. On the front, disorganization and treason rule. Is this the end of socialism and democracy? Are all the effort and work, and to a certain extent even the accomplishments, of the last twenty-four years to be lost? Does France's fate await our country as well? What will become of us?

I am swept along by this sad reality. What should I do? Should I travel from here to a city like Saratov?

Tuesday the 21st of July [1942]

I've already answered the physics questions and studied the entire literature curriculum. I've even been excused from German. Mikhail Ivanovich has promised to abbreviate the history and chemistry courses. It's all well and good, I'm almost a college student.

* City on the Volga north of Stalingrad.

Unfortunately, what's bad is the overall political situation, since we are losing the war. With fear and trembling we listen to the radio every morning. We have already lost Voroshilovgrad, and there's fighting at the gates of Voronezh. There are unofficial reports that Saratov and Kuybyshev have been bombed six times. There are cases of sabotage and treason.

The giant body of the nation and of the country is covered with wounds, and many of its limbs have been severed, the blood gushing forth from its arteries. Many citizens fall under the bombs of enemy air attacks, or from the bullets of the German beasts. Dreadful atrocity! Who can make plans for the future at such a time? Can you cut yourself off from the community and go off into the world to perish? Where to? Why throw yourself into the waves of a stormy ocean when you can't even swim? I've stopped my preparations for departure. I'll finish the tenth grade here!

My mental state is one of deep depression. Not only has nothing come of my plans, but I feel the ground crumbling beneath my feet—the whole country is being destroyed. What will remain of our lives?

Tuesday the 28th of July [1942]

The country is in terrible danger. It's difficult to express the horror that surrounds us. Today the radio announced that our armies have evacuated Novocherkask and Rostov-on-Don. The enemy has reached the Don and is heading for the Volga. The whole Donets coal basin, the iron of Krivoy Rog, are in enemy hands. And on the Black Sea the enemy rules as well. On the entire southern front we suffer constant defeats. On the Western front—all quiet.

When the director came back from a mission to Gorky [Nizhni Novgorod] and learned that I had put a stop to my preparations to depart, he brushed it aside, saying that I had "done the smart thing."

Lately I haven't been feeling too well. I tire easily, have heart palpitations, and feel dizzy. Rebecca Izraelevna gives me a lot of care. She tells the attendants to give me some milk, an egg; she brings me fried fish from the kitchen between breakfast and lunch. She also offers me sweet pickles, fresh carrots, chives, sweet peas. She tries hard to bring me back to health, and she also frees me from a lot of work. She loves me very much, to the point that all the kids have noticed it. I am very grateful to her! She takes the place of my mother, she's a guide, a teacher, a friend! I doubt if I'll ever find such a good friend again, one to whom I could be so attached. The summer days are beautiful now. Work in the children's home has started again: different groups make Sunday excursions to the nearby collective farms, work in the fields and in the garden. They gather medicinal herbs—chamomile, lime-flowers, black currants, nettles—then back to guard duty and the like. Because of my physical condition I take no part in this work. Still I work a bit in administration.

I wish the school year were starting already, but it's still a long way off. It will probably begin the first of October, in other words, in two months. By then it will be autumn, and after that—a fierce winter. Oy!

Friday the 31st of July [1942]

Last night it took me a long time to fall asleep. I tossed from one side of the bed to the other and then got out of bed in the dark, put on my bathrobe, and went out into the courtyard. It was a dark night. The trees on the grounds of the children's home stand quiet and tall like shadows, enclosing the space in a semi-circle. A pale moon shines through the branches and leaves. It's quiet all around: the only sounds are the hissing of the nocturnal moths and other night insects. I sit down on the little bridge, sunk in thought. At my feet lies Sharik, our dog. I look up to the sky—an immense depth and breadth, an infinity, in which my thoughts are scattered. I gather them up with great effort and tie them together into a question that has long tormented my brain: what will my future look like? I once dreamed that I'd be a hero of science, that I would someday write, create. What awaits me now? Another year in Karakulino, at the private village school. And after that? If only this accursed war would end! Then I would be able to attend an institute! Intoxicated by this dream, I return to my room and get back in bed. Was it the pale moon that brought me these thoughts?

Wednesday the 5th of August [1942]

Rebecca Izraelevna worries about me a lot and loves me. She surrounds me with maternal care and special attention. She's like a mother, a teacher, an educator, and a friend: she possesses all these attributes. Fortunately, her glances are focused on me, I'm very touched and pleased. I'm so happy about this treasure, because I'm richer than all my acquaintances. And these acquaintances—the community in which I find myself—are in this sense poorer, and they envy me a lot. Envy is not strong enough a word—they sometimes so provoke me with their barbs that I see stars. The older girls, who are starved for affection and aware of our friendship, are jealous. I notice envious glances and hear sarcastic remarks. Rebecca Izraelevna takes good care of me, just as they used to take care of me. Why have they cut themselves off from me now? Yesterday I was awakened at three in the morning to work at the granary, which I had been excused from doing previously on account of my health. I went with them in the evening, felt unwell and lay down, and no one asked what was the matter. When I say that I'm not well, they make ironic remarks. When Rebecca Izraelevna speaks to me, they look at it askance, making sarcastic jokes about our friendship. Once again I feel bad in the surroundings into which fate has thrust me.

Wednesday the 12th of August [1942]

Last night I strolled along the banks of the Kama. I stood on the shore and stared at the water. Countless waves rush to strike the shore with a playful slap! And the wind sweeps the water away into the distance. Just as the wind drives the water, people are driven by their whole lives. Try to stop, you don't have the strength. How small and insignificant are man and his deeds in comparison to infinity. Small? But how important are his deeds for the others on earth. How much wealth, heroism, strength, and wisdom some people have to offer. Others—baseness. I am reminded of Gorky's "Song of the Falcon" that I recited not long ago:

Bezumstuv khrabikh poiem my slavu!
Ya znaiu shchastie! . . . Ya khrabro bylsya . . . Ya vidyal nebo!

[We sing of the madness of the brave!
I know the good fortune! . . . I fought bravely . . . I saw the sky!]

Like the courageous falcon, I, too, want to see the sky, to lift myself high, see all, know much, so I can teach others. I must study, work on myself. Unfortunately, once again I don't have time. We have to work in the fields. I'd like the school year to begin again. Unfortunately, we still have to wait two months: August and September. The school year begins in October. That will be my second year of school away from home. I want to be in a big city already!

Meanwhile, there's still a bloody war, and on our country's fronts the situation is very sad: bitter fighting around Armavir and near the Kuban River.[*] They are already evacuating everyone from Saratov!

Rodyna v smertelnoi opastnosti. [The motherland is in mortal danger.]

Monday the 31st of August [1942]

Yesterday we had an evening devoted to the memory of Mickiewicz.[†] I gave the lecture on his life and works. I was warmly congratulated for such a successful, serious lecture, which everybody enjoyed. Rebecca Izraelevna even kissed me and gave me a piece of chocolate.

---

[*] In southeastern Russia as the German summer offensive headed for the Caucasus.

[†] Adam Mickiewicz (1798–1855), Polish poet and patriot, was the bard of Polish Romanticism, and remains an icon of Polish culture. Much of his classic work was written while in exile in Russia, to which he was banished for his political activities. His mother was reputedly Jewish. He was an advocate of radical social reform and equality as well as of Polish independence.

Tuesday the 29th of September [1942]

Summer has ended, and with it, the vacation. Day after tomorrow, the new school year begins. And I really do want to go to school and learn! Meanwhile it's a beautiful cold autumn day. Today we finished digging out the potatoes in our field and stored them in the cellar. Two weeks ago we reaped and gathered oats from the field. That's how we were busy, getting ready for winter.

Wednesday the 14th of October [1942]

At last, the dear, long-awaited school-year days have arrived. We have classes from one thirty in the afternoon until five or six in the evening. For me, that's just fine. Until twelve thirty, I prepare for class, spending time with the weaker students at the children's home. I manage also to take care of necessities like sewing, washing my clothes, and so forth.

From seven o'clock in the evening until twelve, I read. But the problem of lighting is worse this year than last. There's almost no kerosene available. And I sit before barely an inkwell's worth of kerosene, though it's a crime against my eyes. But, after all, I can't go to sleep at seven o'clock! The instruction at school is at a higher level this year than last, because of the new teachers who came from Leningrad and Moscow. Since Vladimir Aleksandrovich has been drafted into the army, we have a new homeroom teacher and teacher of mathematics from Leningrad—Antonina Aleksandrovna. She explains things very well and in general presents the subject matter in a very interesting manner. Literature is taught by Anatoly Dimitrevich, also very interestingly. Mikhail Ivanovich does a brilliant job teaching history, along with history of the Communist Party. Nina Vladimirovna teaches chemistry. Nina Moiseyevna has enhanced the teaching of German, and teaches the course in our grade as well. For us it's an achievement. A new subject has also been added—agronomy. For the time being there is no teacher of physics or astronomy. That may yet come.

My mood is fresh and cheerful. I study conscientiously and thoroughly; I read a lot. Recently elections were held for the children's council. The work of the council was rated highly—very gratifying! The director unleashed his two pets, Lyuboshitsky and Khonon Khazanovich, against me. Lyuboshitsky publicly insulted me, with "his" permission. As a result, I withdrew my candidacy for the council, though I haven't given up my communal activities. I work on the Study Committee and the Cultural Committee. I'm very pleased that I have nothing more to do with the director. Rebecca Izraelevna has moved away from our division (where she lived until now) to live with Olga Vladimirovna, the wife of Vladimir Aleksandrovich. Now I see her only in the dining room, where we hardly speak, and it pains me. I would visit her in the evening if I knew that it wouldn't disturb her. At her place, there's bound to be light! Today she said to me with a smile, "How seldom we see each other!" In the past, we used to converse every evening. Now I am deeply involved in my work, and she in hers. Our mutual activity (work on the council) has come to an end.

I felt that she regretted that things were this way, but that she lacked the boldness to invite me over. But I guess I'll go see her this evening. It's funny! I want the year to be over quickly, so I can work on a collective farm during the summer. Like Genya—to provide myself with food and some money, so that I'll be able to go away to study.

After vacation time, at the end of September, I started to write a short story in Russian. I don't write in Yiddish because I have nobody to write for . . . to my great regret! Nobody knows about my work. For the time being I'm telling no one, because I haven't finished and there's nothing to show yet. My heroine is a sixteen-year-old girl who is evacuated from her home at the outbreak of the war.[*]

Tuesday the 27th of October [1942]

Classes are still not back to normal. First of all, we are still missing a teacher of physics and astronomy; and second, we're

[*] This may be a reference to the story "Mirl"(which Lena never completed) that precedes the diary (see p. 1).

often torn away from our studies and sent to work on a collective farm. Today, for example, classes have already been interrupted; tomorrow we're going to the collective farm. Tanya, who has gone off to Izhevsk to study medicine, complains about her situation: she has to do a lot of work apart from her studies.

Why is the world full of injustice, baseness? Why, why?

Wednesday the 28th of October [1942]

Rebecca Izraelevna will no longer be working for us. In accordance with an order from the Narkompros, she was removed from her job. The director fought with her all summer, gathered signatures from the counselors stating that she is not a help to them, took along Khonon to Izhevsk, and the two of them defeated her. What a false, base way to behave! She knew too much about how much food, merchandise, and clothing that was being bought went to him and his family and to those he wanted to bribe and flatter! Now Berta Pavlovna will be selected to replace Rebecca Izraelevna. Fanny and Berta Pavlovna's parents have recently come to us from Leningrad. They're all relatives of the director. Rebecca Izraelevna has been left without work. I don't know yet what arrangements she'll make. Perhaps work with the district library and teach German at our school? Rebecca Izraelevna has been deeply affected by this disgrace, but she's holding up well. For me it is a great pity. After all, she is my dear, good, wise friend! She was ruthlessly punished, because she fell into the hands of an unjust person. Helena Pantelemonovna also wants to leave, but the director will not let her go under any circumstances.

Tuesday the 10th of November [1942], 9:00 in the morning

Finally, the art of living has been made clear to me: the struggle for existence, adapting to circumstances no matter how difficult, accepting fate, and trying to make better arrangements for tomorrow. I've become accustomed to sleeping in a cold room—at the children's home right now we have no wood—twisting myself like a bagel and not shutting an eye, because the blood is congealing in my veins. I do not react to events such as doing homework in a broken chair, or writing with my hands blue and swollen from the cold! Or when, as often happens, the midday meal is not ready by twelve or one o'clock and we go to school without having eaten, or when there are only 250 grams of bread in my stomach—150 grams from breakfast and 100 grams at midday. For the entire day, all we get is 400 grams of bread. That does not astonish me. We have little kerosene as well, which is why we can't read in the evening, since we have no light. What can we do? It's the second year of the war. There are no better prospects in view.

At the front the situation is also very depressing. So far, our allies have not yet opened a second front. The southern Soviet Union is already in German hands—parts of the Caucasus, the shores of the Black Sea. The enemy has succeeded in capturing important oil fields: Maykop, Tuapse, Nal'chik. For quite a few weeks there's been bitter fighting in the streets of Stalingrad. Hitler wants to cut off the Volga and seize this broad highway of bread and oil. The country wheezes and struggles, defending itself with all its strength, not sparing even great sacrifice. The country is starving and freezing. Thousands of people—workers in the factories—don't even have the minimum of food, which we have. Thousands would envy us our midday meal, which consists of simple potatoes, without fat or salt. A pud of potatoes costs 600 rubles at the market. For us, at least, they grow in the garden. Sometimes we even get a microscopic piece of meat!

Tanya wrote to us that Genya feels very desperate about her situation. She has settled in a good neighborhood, but it's very hard for her financially: she has to wait in line three to four hours for bread and a midday meal. At the university, lectures are not going normally, because there are not enough professors. The food supplies she had brought along from her work are almost used up. She has no more money, and they're not giving out scholarships. She wants to become a blood donor, because donors get more to eat. If that doesn't work out, she will take work in a factory.

This is my perspective on the coming year: perhaps things will be even worse, because it seems that the war won't be ending so fast.

The third year of war is always much worse than the second year.

Rebecca Izraelevna was left out on the street—without work. There's no possibility at all of her getting accommodations here. Maybe she'll go soon to her son's and settle there.

This is how the Soviet reality looks today: extremely harsh. Still, we want to live, to hope for a better new morning, for a nice, sunny day! I live and learn, so that I may live and work.

Wednesday the 18th of November [1942]

I want to preserve a picture of my life, my daily routine: I get up at seven in the morning, when it's still dark. At half past seven I eat breakfast, and until half past eight I help the backward pupils do their homework. At nine o'clock classes begin. Until three o'clock I'm in school. At three o'clock we have the midday meal. From half past three until six o'clock I do my homework. Nine o'clock is supper. From half past six until eleven or twelve I read. Sometimes I visit with Helena Pantelemonovna, sometimes with girls from my class. Sometimes there are meetings in the children's home. Sunday we saw wood for the kitchen and for the dormitory for the whole week.

I'm beginning to master the art of life. I adapt to circumstances, perform daily physical chores, and study. Recently I have become convinced that I've bent the twig too far—gone too far away into the land of books, turned myself into a bookworm. Now I'm coming back to earth, not as a worm that crawls, but as a human being, who, without losing her bearing, walks firmly on the ground, yet holds her head up to the sky.

Sunday the 29th of November [1942], 9:30 in the evening

Slowly the last few hours of my eighteenth year are expiring. Soon my eighteenth year will come to an end. A year without parents, without friends or close comrades, in a foreign land during a time of bloody war and famine. Along with it, my childhood and early youth have also come to an end. By law I'm no longer a minor. I am an adult who will have the right to vote, the right to work and an education; a citizen of the Soviet Union, who bears full responsibility for her actions, and from whom work, exertion, and discipline are demanded. I am responsible for my actions, it is no longer my parents! I must go through life myself and build my future. My entire future life depends on my energy, endurance, and will! If I lived in normal, peaceful circumstances, surrounded by my family, I might perhaps face different duties and prospects. But what is the point of contemplating what might have been under those circumstances? I do not have my family now. Will I ever see them? Who knows . . . if I'll ever again see my dear, good mother, my poor father, my little sister, and my brother. Would they be able to understand me and guide me to a path in life? My mother—that kind, wise, and self-sacrificing woman of the people—didn't understand me two years ago, when I was still at home. The same with the other members of my family.

My path in life, though quite hazy and uncertain, I chose when I was thirteen, when at the price of strenuous work and study I pulled myself out of the class to which my family belongs—simple proletarians—and created a path for myself to the intelligentsia. Now four years have passed. The distance between us is enormous. In my heart there remains a deep feeling of gratitude and love, a desire to repay them for having formed me. I understand them, but they cannot understand me. After all, they are too far away. The conflict that might have arisen has been avoided. I have been left alone. I've matured a lot lately. Life has thrown me into various situations, taught me much. At first I trembled in desperation whenever storm winds whipped my heart. Now I've become used to it, and a storm is not so terrifying. Despite the burden of my financial worries, and the fact that I find myself in a community of children (the oldest only sixteen or seventeen years old), still I see clearly the world around me, well understand human relationships, the demands and laws of life. I know that I'll find happiness in strenuous, unceasing work, constantly adapting myself to circumstances, moving swiftly on the wheel of history.

For if I stop for an instant, my mind will be ground to pieces. Better less looking back to the past, speculating about the fine nuances of feelings, experiences, moods! Less slipping off into the world of sweet dreams about the future, a world that exists only in fantasy! As much as possible, I must think, work, and live in today. Today, I am still a student in the tenth grade of high school, being raised in a children's home. Today I have to study, read, acquire knowledge, and observe life so that eight or nine months from now I can independently go out into the battle I want to win. To learn to live is more than learning from books. First and foremost, you must learn from life as well! From that perspective!

With such thoughts I begin my nineteenth year.

Thursday the 3rd of December [1942]

I've just finished reading Lion Feuchtwanger's[*] *The Jewish War*. I cannot recall another book that has had as much of an effect on me. This book has led me back to the world from which I've been torn away for several years. The history of my ancestors, my people, from whom I am now so distant, has been reawakened. I'm reminded of the lectures in Jewish history by my teacher Mr. Katz and it hurts me that I'll never hear them again. Before my eyes once more I see the Temple, Jerusalem besieged, thousands of heroic defenders who died as martyrs, famished, thirsty, with eyes that knew no sleep or rest. They stood on the walls of Jerusalem and hurled huge stones and poured molten tar on the heads of the Roman legionnaires. Afterward—the Temple in flames, the altar splashed with human blood, the torn Torah scroll. Titus's triumphal procession and thousands of prisoners in chains, the masses of jeering Romans, licking their chops with pleasure at the sight of Jewish prisoners in gladiatorial combat at the Coliseum. Then

---

[*] The German-Jewish novelist Lion Feuchtwanger (1884–1958) wrote a trilogy based on the life of the early Jewish historian Josephus Flavius (37–c. 100 C.E.).

Judea was finally destroyed, only ash and ruins left, hundreds of people burned [*sic*] on the cross and the final "*Shema Yisroel*" falling from their self-sacrificing, parched lips. Overlooking this scene, the son of Israel, Josephus Flavius, Yosef ben Matityahu, hero and traitor, the *kohen* [Hebrew: biblical priest] and historian, a man who wanted to unite the wisdom of the Jewish East with the culture of the rising West—Rome's humanism, organization, discipline, and the heritage of Greek Hellenism. How complicated is the psychology of this cultured, clever, talented, capable Jew!

At the outset a Maccabean, a leader of the Jewish rebels, a *kohen* of the first rank! Thereafter, Vespasian's prisoner, his prophet, despised and degraded, who unites the brilliance and riches of the court of Caesar with the sound of rusty chains, with the basest insults and mockery of Caesar. On the other hand, a branded traitor to the Jewish people, who excommunicated him and whose brethren by blood avoid him like the plague.

Josephus Flavius, the genius who stands on the borderline between two cultures, two peoples, despised and misunderstood by both, who more than anyone understood what superhuman suffering felt like—it was his fate to see Jerusalem fall, to witness, from the imperial box, Titus's triumph and the leaders of his own heroic nation in chains. It was his lot to transmit to the coming generations the history of the heroic struggle. He wrote in Greek: "I have decided to describe the war as it was, so the public may be reminded of it and the coming generations may be apprised."

It may be that Josephus's fate will be long remembered. It is hard to defend him for his betrayal, but even harder to blame. One can understand Josephus and sympathize with him.

A thought steals into my mind: Am I not also betraying my people if I move away to a very different culture?

Sunday the 20th of December [1942]

When I look back over my recent and distant past, it seems to me so very naïve, childish, half-fantastic, and unreal. Yesterday

I was still a deluded child, seeing nothing of what was around me! Yesterday I still believed that books are everything, that life meant only studying. Consequently, I did nothing besides study, and required only the conditions necessary for study. For that reason I had no idea of the conditions in which everyone else lived—that is, adults who lived outside the framework of the children's home. Now I'm beginning to understand: now I've recognized the struggle for existence, for bread, for firewood, and so forth. Only now do I notice the different life circumstances, for example, of Helena Pantelemonovna: a young, talented artist, who doesn't even have a chance to develop her talent; and despite the fact that she's working, she and her two-year-old child are dying of hunger. Similarly, Rebecca Izraelevna, who works as a teacher in our school, barely manages on what she earns. Fanny and B[erta] P. now live with their parents in affluence and ease, despite the fact that it's wartime and millions are starving. The first two suffer because they cannot wheel and deal, they're open, honest, tread the straight and narrow. The other two are greedy, have no feelings for other people. So their lives are better!

In order to live you have to come down from the sky! That's what circumstances teach me. Now I want to learn not only from books, but more from life! I want to drink from the fountain of life, know the taste of passions and feelings, I want to feel what they call happiness. I want to live! What lies ahead for me? I know that I'll construct my life myself, and everything will depend on how I'll deal with circumstances!

Friday the 1st of January [1943]

It's three in the morning. We're all exhausted from long hours of dancing, singing, playing. But nobody wants to admit it and go to sleep. All the laughter is tired and artificial, the young voices loud. It's time to greet the new year. The year 1942 has already joined the chain of history. An entire year in the Udmurtian village of Karakulino, in a home for refugee children. A whole year of war and bloodletting, a harsh wartime year. What will the year 1943 bring to us and to humankind? I begin the year in Karakulino. Where will the year end? Will this year bring us peace and victory, as we want to believe, and as many assure us? Will it bring me rewarding activities and recognition?

The year is only three hours old. What does it carry on its innocent white wings? Perhaps its songs are already soiled with the blood of fallen heroes, soiled with the bitter tears of tortured women, children, and old people in Hitler-land? Maybe its angelic face is distorted by the pain from my mother's tears over my violated sister and castrated brother? I should like to believe in and hope for better things! Everyone thirsts for happiness.

Year 1943—end this war!

Tick-tock! From Gorky's *Hours*.

In the solitude and silence of the night it's unpleasant to hear the not-terribly-nice words about the events of our time; the monotonous and mathematically correct sounds, always pretentiously signifying the same thing: the eternal movement of life!

Thursday the 21st of January [1943]

I haven't had a letter from Genya for a long time. In her last letter she wrote that she's horrified at the prospect of being a teacher. So she's trying to transfer to an institute of medicine in Izhevsk. She's written the same thing to Tanya. But moving to Izhevsk is fraught with difficulties, so now she wants to go to Sverdlovsk. Now they're all looking eagerly at me: What will I do? I'm thinking of applying to the literature faculty at Kazan University. It's still too early to make a plan, but various ideas come into my head. I want to study literature, learn languages on my own. But why dream? It's been a while since I started to write a story in Russian. I have great hopes for it, though I do not write often, because I don't have any time. As a matter of fact, I believe too much in my own powers. Maybe it's because I feel that many people regard me highly. Sometimes I think that I have in me a spark of that fire known as talent. At times I think that I should study in a drama school. Recently in Karakulino I recited, to great acclaim, an excerpt from Wanda Wasilewska's *Rainbow*, as well as several poems devoted to the Patriotic War.* All the teachers and exiled intellectuals wait impatiently for my performances. Many are jealous of me—most of all Shura Zlatina, but also Vera Furmanski, who quietly tries to imitate me in everything, along with other girls from our dormitory. What should I make of this, what shall I choose for my profession? Should I go with my dream?

Sunday the 31st of January [1943]

There are days that bring me great joy, carry something new into my gray life. My teachers Antonina Alexandrovna—the mathematics teacher—and Nina Moiseyevna—our homeroom teacher and German teacher—are very friendly toward me, far more than with the other students. They speak all the time about my gifts. Fate has robbed me of many things: my parents were not rich people, not very educated. So from my earliest years I knew what it felt like to be poor. Now I know what it feels like to be lonely. But I have been blessed with abilities! How should I develop these gifts in order to serve society? Lately I think a lot about my future profession. Where to? Perhaps I'm now under the influence of practical people? That's possible. Should I then study to be an engineer? That could assure me of a better material situation and tie me closer to a practical life. So I'll stop building castles in the air. And such a choice would not exclude any further intellectual activity. After all, you can be a good engineer and still be interested in literature and languages. Does the one necessarily exclude the other? No! I must build an economic foundation for myself, because whatever I do not acquire by myself, nobody will give me. My parents, too, lived in poverty and want, wearing hand-me-downs. My mother couldn't appear in society, and neither could my father, because

---

* Wanda Wasilewska (1905–1964), Polish novelist and leftist political activist. During and after World War II (known as the Patriotic War) she lived in the Soviet Union. *Raduga* (Rainbow) reflects on life in a Nazi-occupied village in Ukraine. It was also made into a Soviet film.

they had no decent clothes. We children lived for several years in charitable institutions. I do not ask for riches, but I don't want to be a beggar anymore!

Wednesday the 3rd of February [1943]

But now I am a beggar all the same! Fate, why? Why so poor? The most painful thing of all is that other people notice it and look down at me, as they do at all the inmates of the children's home. My clothes, which were not the newest to begin with, are becoming more and more torn . . . and no new ones are coming in. Lucky that I live in a village, where the local children also aren't noted for their elegant dress. Still, here there's now quite a large group of refugees from the big cities, who are relatively well dressed. What will happen half a year from now, when I will show up in a city to study?

Fanny Pavlovna, my kindly counselor, now lives in luxury and riches and therefore looks down on me. She well knows our circumstances, sees how greedy we are when we carry our bowls to supplement the watery soup with a spoonful of kasha. I'm not complaining. After all, for the time being, I have to make peace with my circumstances; but our stomachs are never full, though they try to convince us that we live well compared to others during wartime. Sometimes I feel like visiting one of my acquaintances because I know that they'll offer me something to eat: a few potatoes, a piece of bread, perhaps some salad. From time to time I make an effort to fight this craftiness, but I don't always succeed. I feel most uncomfortable when I'm at Fanny Pavlovna's, and her mother starts serving food. I know that all this maternal cordiality and hospitality stems only from the fact that she needs me: Shura is taking math and needs my help! It's all a question of relationships and circumstances! I don't want to cut off my assistance to Shura. In general, I like it when people admire and count on me. When I compare myself to Shura—though she has her mother, grandmother, and grandfather, nice clothes, and a lot to eat, but is dull and silly—

I come to the conclusion that I'm much better off, and I wouldn't want to trade places with her!

I believe that with my own strength I can build my life. In connection with that I've even changed my plans concerning further education and specialization. I've come to the conclusion that you can always study up on literature, if you want to read, and have the time and interest. In life you have to find a specialty that will secure your economic foundation. Therefore, I've decided to finish school and go on to a technical institute to study engineering, perhaps even in Izhevsk.

Thursday the 11th of February [1943]

Antonina Aleksandrovna, our homeroom teacher and math teacher, proposed that I learn French, although according to her specialty she is not a linguist. But she has found a book and has started to teach me. I put together syllables with great effort, but I hope soon to be able to read French!

Fate has once again smiled sweetly at me: Shura Zlatina has to take her exams with the rest of the class, but she is in great despair. Fanny Pavlovna has asked me to prepare Shura for the math and physics exams, and at the same time promised to help me in my pursuits as an independent student. She is sugar-sweet to me, calling me "Lenusinka."

Thursday the 29th of April [1943]

I am now facing the second spring far from home: it's already warm, bright, dry. And my mood is exactly like nature! Recently I've gotten a new, green summer coat, and a green silk dress—a partial wardrobe for my independent student life! My relationship with the director has greatly improved, I've found favor with the secretary of the *Raikom* [district committee] of the Party, who praises me highly for my knowledge and has even asked me to go dancing in the evening. Not long ago it was Passover, and Fanny

Pavlovna's mother invited me to their seder! All in all, they live very well and often treat me to fine foods like bread and butter, sweet tea, fish, and salad, which are now luxuries. At Passover I even ate matzo, an egg, honey cake, and torte! When I visit them, I'm reminded of the old, traditional Jewish families, and it pains me that I no longer have a home.

Exams are approaching in all thirteen class subjects. I'm preparing gradually, but not completely, because I'm still without my glasses. And second, a lot of my time is taken up with rehearsals. Soon we'll be putting on Katayev's* *The Blue Handkerchief*, in which I play the main character, Dasha.

On the fourteenth of April we received a telegram from Stalin with thanks for the 10,000 rubles that we donated to the Defense Front. The day was a very happy one! It's no small matter. Stalin thanked us in the name of the Red Army! All day long we celebrated, sang, and danced.

Saturday the 22nd of May [1943]

I've just come from the exam in Russian literature. Today we had the oral exam. Thursday was the written. My essay, "The Russian Woman According to Gorky's *Mother*," was rated higher than "excellent" and made a great impression on the teachers. The next five exams are in math. I'm already well prepared. Soon I'll have to think about leaving. Where to? I want to go to Moscow. Genya has already transferred there along with her exiled university.

Friday the 11th of June [1943]

This is how I finished school: yesterday at three in the afternoon I took my last exam in German.

Today I am already a graduate. On the fourteenth the school year ends, and there will be an evening graduation ceremony, when I'll receive my diploma. Now I am trying to start working. Right after the

---

* Valentin Petrovich Katayev (1897–1986), popular Russian novelist and playwright, known for his humorous treatment of the problems of Soviet society.

exams I went to see Mikhail Ivanovich, the director of "Sono,"[*]and asked him to arrange work for me in the collective farm's kindergarten, so that I can earn flour for the summer. He promised. I don't know how it will work out, since this year there are few kindergartens and many teachers who want to work. A lot of our teachers asked him even before I did. Still, he did promise me. If I succeed in working here, I'll be very pleased!

Tuesday the 29th of June [1943]

A long time has gone by and I still haven't arranged for work. The kindergarten to which I've been assigned is not yet in operation. But thanks to a friend of mine, I succeeded in finding work in the *kolkhoz* [collective farm] Ilyich[†] in the village of Maragino, 6 kilometers from here. I'll be working in the tractor driver department. The work is very hard and a serious responsibility: I'll be responsible for the kerosene, benzene, and other fuels that in wartime are so important. I'll have to live in the fields and walk a lot in order to measure how much land the tractor drivers have plowed. On the other hand, the wages are very good: 6 kilo of flour a day! In today's prices, that's 600 rubles. They say that the tractor drivers are fed very well. And that, too, is very important! Lately the food in the children's home has been very meager. At eight o'clock in the morning, 200 grams of bread, 10 grams of butter, 10 grams of sugar. All of this will by no means satisfy a shrunken, famished stomach. At three in the afternoon, a bowl of *shchav* [sorrel soup] or soup with nettles, in which you can sometimes find half a small potato and a spoonful of kasha. After this midday meal, everyone leaves the table even more disappointed than before the meal; our hopes to ease the cramps in our half-empty stomachs have run out like a cracked egg. At seven in the evening, 200 grams of bread, a glass of milk, and again two spoonfuls of kasha—if we're lucky! Once in a while, a tenth of a small fish, a quarter of an omelette. I have lost 10 kilos recently. All in all, no day goes by when I'm able to forget my stomach.

[*] Abbreviation for a government agency.
[†] Named for Vladimir Ilyich Lenin.

Unfortunately, I'm losing my strength, but I approach my work with great interest. I want to meet the people and work alongside them. I hope that in the open country I will strengthen and fortify myself a bit—and perhaps forget about my stomach. I'll also earn bread there and ensure my economic survival for the winter, for the time when I'll begin my studies. So—to work tomorrow! Maragino!

Friday the 2nd of July [1943]

Dressed in long flannel pants, a boy's sweater given to me by one of the boys at the children's home, a kerchief on my head, hemp shoes wrapped in cloth, I live in the midst of the fields, not far from Karakulino, in the village of Maragino. I work in the tractor driver section. My job is to distribute and supervise fuels, keep records on how much each tractor driver has plowed, how much kerosene he has used, and how many workdays he's completed. The work is not hard, but it is responsible.

I'm sitting for the second day in the wagon where twelve tractor drivers live. I hear the young peasant boys curse, I watch them repair the machines. I have a lot of free time. I pick berries, I read, I dream. At night I sleep at a peasant woman's house in the village, but sometimes I end up staying in the wagon. Today, for example, I slept on a plank cot with my head against a post and an adding machine, shivering from the cold because my blanket was back in the village.

Saturday the 3rd of July [1943]

Again an entire day in the wagon. At night it is very cold, and I can't go to the village because the tractors are filled with kerosene at night. I feel very bad. My head and stomach hurt, and the worst curse words ring in my ears, eating into my brain like pesky flies. Where can I run to? It seems to me that I won't last long here, I'll run away. Oh! At night in my bed in Karakulino, where it was soft, warm, and comfortable, I used to quietly calculate how many puds of flour I'd earn in summer and then I'd do "Menachem-Mendl"[*] business deals. The only thing that keeps me in this filth is the awareness that it's necessary for my further studies. This is a sacrifice that I make for my education. In order to exist somehow next year and not perish of hunger, I have to earn my bread now! In addition, I'm preparing myself to struggle with the hardships I encounter. Who knows what fate has yet in store for me. Who knows in what conditions I'll have to live? The main thing is not to become discouraged and to endure!

Thursday the 8th of July [1943]

When I left with my accounts for the office of the MTS[†] on Monday, I also stopped in at the children's home. There they all enveloped me, and tried to help in some way—Vera in particular. She gathers together my documents and sends them out to those institutes I request. I am very, very grateful to her. In general, I was very touched by the warmth that was displayed toward me. Everybody asked about my work, about everything. I hadn't yet spoken with the director, because he was not at home. When he arrived, he told me that tomorrow they're putting on *The Blue Handkerchief,* in which I play the main role. They decided that I should ask my work-brigade leader to release me for the evening! He released me. I went on foot from the fields to Karakulino—8 km—and began to prepare for the performance. But the performance did not take place, although all of us were in costume and makeup. At two in the morning I went to bed at the children's home. At nine in the morning, after breakfast, I went back to the fields on foot. I was very exhausted and hungry, because the breakfast there was meager and my stomach was empty. I had

[*] Menachem Mendl, a character in works of the great Yiddish humorist Sholem Aleichem, is constantly trying (and failing) to make money through fantastic business schemes.

[†] Machine Tractor Station: In Soviet agriculture, the tractors and other machinery used by collective farmers were government property and were leased from special "stations" that served a group of farms.

hoped that I might find some food and maybe also get some rest. But my illusions ran out like water from a bucket full of holes.

The brigade leader reproached me for coming late. He also told me to order machine oil and travel by myself to the director of the MTS to have him confirm it. I immediately went back to the village, to the chairman of the collective farm, to get a horse and driver. But I couldn't find a driver. So, I stand there helplessly next to the horse, and I'm angry with myself for being helpless. What should I do? What can I do with an animal standing in the harness to make it go? I was nearly in tears. But I sat down in the wagon—and drove off. The horse turns this way and that way, and I pull the reins first to one side, then to the other. Now I'm in a good mood. Aha, I think, how much better my situation is now! When I was already close to Karakulino it started to rain. I managed to tie the horse to a pole and went right to the director. He granted the request. Now it started to pour! I had to sit and wait until it ended. During that time the horse fell, and I thought he had broken a foot. He needs to be unharnessed, but I don't know how to do it. A few women came to help me, and they got wet.

After the downpour came to an end, I went to the children's home to get something to put on and also to eat. I was touched once again by the warmth that enveloped me. One of the boys put the horse back in harness, and I went off to the fuel depot. But here I faced a new calamity: there's a rule that whoever arrives to pick up fuel must transfer ten barrels of fuel from one depot to the other. What a bother! Again I ran to the director of the MTS to ask him to relieve me of this obligation. "In your bad luck you also have to have good luck," says Motl Peysi* the cantor's son. He relieved me. Now I am back in the fields, after spending the whole day like that.

This morning it rained again. The tractors drove off late.

The same day—in the afternoon.

When I came to sleep at the woman's house in the village, I noticed that my pillow had no pillowcase. I understood that the peas-

---

* Young hero of Sholem Aleichem's novel of the same name.

ant woman had removed it. I asked her for it, and she gave me back the pillowcase. But from time to time she grumbles. If I wash my feet before going to bed, that's an issue for her. When I brought a sheet from the children's home for my bed, that's her affair as well. Will she take it, too? Her daughter is a cook who works for us, and she cleans up at our expense: bread, kasha, milk, and meat. It seems to me that she first removes the cream from the milk, unfortunately!

Friday the 9th of July [1943]

My life working in the fields is becoming more stressful by the day. Despite the fact that I treat the tractor drivers very well, greet them with a friendly word and a smile, they treat me badly. First of all, they think that I don't do anything: doling out and measuring the fuel for everyone, writing it down—that's not work. Second, it's because I'm Jewish. (Who says that there is no anti-Semitism here?) Third, because I wash my hands before eating and eat with my own spoon. Most important of all, because unlike the female tractor drivers, I won't let them embrace me. True, not all of them behave badly. There are two hateful creatures here—boys of fourteen and fifteen. Just now they tore down a chart from the wall, which is very important for my work, and smoked it instead of cigarettes. Already twice they've poured machine oil in my cup. They curse constantly: Jew, Jew! Because of this, my work becomes all the more difficult. But I strain every nerve in order to persevere: I have to earn bread for my studies at any cost!

Saturday the 10th of July [1943]

Yesterday we completed the 24-hectare area and started a new one. For that reason we moved the wagon over. Now we are 5 kilometers from the village. To walk there and back twice a day is no great pleasure, but what can we do? That's what the work demands. Generally, I've been doing a lot more walking. I have to walk around the whole field measuring how much the tractor has plowed. Today I've already been to the MTS in Karakulino (11 kilo-meters from the fields in each direction) with the accounts, and I am exhausted. But I have to confess: I've already gotten a bit used to it—otherwise I wouldn't be about to go pick berries. All in all, the work would be tolerable (though filthy), if not for the "society." If they were adults, it would certainly be better. These are young hooligans. I try hard not to pay attention to them. I remember only that I have to earn bread for my studies.

As always, I wait impatiently for the day when I have to go to Karakulino with the accounts. I usually stop off at the children's home for a few hours. I am received most cordially. I wash up there, hear the latest news, and get a break from the local crowd. Today my brigade leader didn't allow me to linger, telling me to return to the fields right away. I just managed to show my face at the children's home; but I didn't find Berta Pavlovna or Samuil Markovich and had to go back immediately. I've noticed that many of the older children envy me. First of all, I have enough food to eat while they—as usual—still go hungry. Second, I will be earning flour! Even the teachers are envious and call me jokingly "a rich lady"! They silently calculate how many puds I have earned and will earn in the future. A pud of flour now costs more than 2,000 rubles at the market! I'm counting, too. According to my reckoning, in the past ten days I earned three puds.

I've sent applications to six schools: Kazan University, Kazan Medical Institute, Izhevsk Medical Institute, Sverdlovsk Institute of Mechanical Engineering, and in Moscow, the Bauman Technical Institute. Who will accept me and where will I go? I don't know yet—time will tell. Meanwhile, I have to keep the fuel accounts and listen to curse words from some tractor drivers.

Sunday the 11th of July [1943]

In the collective farm there is no bread, and we all sit around hungry. In the morning I drank two glasses of buttermilk and ate a few scallions. Afterward, the brigade leader sent me to Karakulino for oil to lubricate the machines. He has become very strict lately. There's a lot of work: we have to walk a lot! And I am very exhausted. I had dinner at the children's home and got a bit of bread. Now I wanted to eat it with butter that I had gotten at the children's home. When I looked in the cupboard I nearly fainted: the cupboard was empty! Everything that I'd brought yesterday was stolen and eaten by one of the tractor drivers! Each of them has milk, cheese, baked goods called *shanges* at home. But, that didn't stop them from taking my food.

When I was at the children's home, I found out that news arrived that Genya's parents are now in Palestine and living together with relatives of Rebecca Izraelevna. For Genya—great joy! Where is my family? Who knows if they are even alive?

All of Job's troubles have happened to me: "Job did not hold out—he became even more miserable," says the accusing angel in the Peretz's *Bontshe Shvayg*. That's how I feel.

Monday the 12th of July [1943]

I've become convinced lately that the war is reflected more in the countryside than anywhere else. In the entire village you cannot find a single adult peasant, except for Sanka the simpleton. All the burden of work is borne on the shoulders of the women and youth aged fourteen to seventeen. There is a shortage of workers. Only children do the plowing: on the tractors, fourteen-, fifteen-, sixteen-year-olds; on horses, even ten-year-olds. They don't plow deep, just any old way. Usually there's no time to plow twice, so the harvest is meager. Not to mention the fact that they don't manage to plow all the soil, or to harvest all the crops at the end of summer. That's why there is so much hunger in the land! That's why we have rations and ration cards even in the countryside and in the army. The collective farms are very poor, and now, just before the new harvest, there's already not enough bread. The collective farm women are very poor, very dissatisfied, and they say that previously, before there were collective farms, things were a lot better! The village is far from patriotic and sings the same old songs from the First World War. In fact, I have not yet heard one Soviet song here.

I understand why: the collective farmer hasn't received any bread since 1937. The collective farm owes many debts to the state, and there is not even the hope of any bread. The farmer feeds himself only with what he gets from his own cow. For his milk, cream, and butter he buys flour, soap, matches, and groceries. Those who have no cow feed themselves only with their bread ration and potatoes from their garden. Gradually all hopes for a swift end to the war and an improvement in their situation have been shattered.

On the front, there's no encouraging news for the time being. The enemy has once again begun a counterattack. In reports on the radio (which, unfortunately, I have no opportunity to hear, and learn about only when I visit the children's home), there are announcements of bombings and attacks on the Finnish front. Who knows how it will turn out this summer? The country has no more strength to fight, and the war is still far from over. It's already the third year of the war. Now it's very, very hard to live. What will happen later? I still have a lot of will and energy to lead an independent life, when I'll be studying. This I must achieve, at any cost! In the hard struggle for existence you must be strong, endure! The difficulties that I now encounter at work are trivial, the unpleasantness created by my fellow workers are silly, compared to the compensation that I receive. In the course of the first month I can earn nine puds of bread (if I get it!), and today that's quite a lot! To the question that people ask me, "How are things at work?" I answer, "Good!" I run around, get a bit tired, sleep little, but I'm satisfied with the work. I have about two more months to work, that is, until two weeks before my departure.

Thursday the 15th of July [1943]

It seems to me that the days are dragging very slowly: I get up before dawn and return to the children's home when it's already quite dark. My working day lasts nineteen hours. True, during the day I can often take a nap, but that's not restful sleep: I doze off, and I hear the roar of the tractors, arriving for their supply of fuel. Often it happens that during the day I have to go back to the village

(5 kilometers away), and from time to time to Karakulino for machine oil.

The time creeps along like a turtle, and I count the days from one accounting day to the next. Sometimes I wonder: Have I really been working only twelve days? Even less than two weeks! It seems that I've been working for a long time. I'm pleased that I have to harden myself for independent living, master the art of what's called the struggle for life, so that I can be an experienced fighter. My current job is not a bad school.

When the brigade leader goes away and all the tractors are working, when I have some free time, I leave the stinking, filthy wagon for the nearby valley to pick berries, roll around in the green grass, look up at the infinity of the sky, and dream. The whole valley is blanketed with sunlight. The tips of the many nearby hills are bathed in golden rays. If I come a little closer and peer into the vegetation, I see the juicy red berries. Here it's so spacious and free! Fields, meadows, plowed soil—the buzz of crickets and other insects. The collective farm's herd grazes in the distance. Poets call this "the palace of nature."

Willy-nilly there come to mind descriptions of nature from literature. I compare it a bit to Sholokhov's *And Quiet Flows the Don*, Gladkov's *Earth*, with Boleslaw Prus's *Placowka*, and Reymont's *The Peasants*.[*] Until now, these descriptions were foreign to me, and I could only imagine a picture full of succulent fresh colors. Now I feel it with my soul. I breathe in deeply the aroma of the fields. Now I've become more closely acquainted with the peasant's arduous life, and I understand his devotion to the land. Now I understand the metaphor "mother earth." How much sweat from sunburned brows does the earth soak up before she bears our

---

[*] Mikhail Sholokhov (1905–1984), Soviet novelist, best known for his descriptions of Cossack life. He was awarded the Nobel Prize for literature in 1965.

Fedor Vasilevich Gladkov (1883–1958), called the first Soviet novelist. A Yiddish translation of his writings *Naye Erd* (New Earth) appeared in Warsaw in 1934.

Boleslaw Prus (1847–1912), Polish novelist and short story writer. *Placowka* (Outpost) was published in 1896.

Wladyslaw Reymont (1868–1925), Polish novelist, best known for his multi-volume epic, *The Peasants*, for which he was awarded the Nobel Prize in 1924.

bread? In plowing, whether with a horse or a tractor (both forms of energy are now in use), the peasant expends much effort on the soil. Then, harrow, replow, cultivate, sow, reap, winnow, thresh, grind. Not one free minute, no rest. The same thing year-in, year-out. The generations change, the social order has changed, but life has changed very little, perhaps only assumed slightly different forms. The work is just as arduous, and that is the secret of famine in wartime. The peasant's living conditions are as dirty as before. He eats unwashed, sleeps on the ground in his clothes, goes about in rags, not colorfully dressed as before. He gets up in the morning to daily worries about his work, about the cow and the pigs, about the garden and food. He goes to bed when it's already dark in order to get some rest after the hard day's work. That's how the peasant lives, that's how the village breathes—without culture. There are many illiterates. Most of the youth have finished only three to five grades.

This picture is altogether unlike its ostensible reflection in literature and art. "Life has become merry, food has become nonexistent," so laughs the peasant about his fate. I experienced my first disappointment two years ago in Sarapul. My current observations are links in the chain of my knowledge of life. Still, nature is extraordinarily beautiful, truly divine. The sun is willing and charming, life is good, interesting, and hard. The contrast between man and nature is immense!

Friday the 16th of July [1943]

It seems that I never felt the pleasure of exhaustion as much as I did last night. Tiredness penetrates my limbs; the soles of my feet are burning, and move forward mechanically. In the evening I walk from the fields to the village. I have to notify the chairman of the collective farm to send a horse and wagon and a coachman early in the morning to deliver fuel from the Karakulino depot. In addition I have to go to the village council to inform the MTS by telephone about the amount of acreage plowed today. Then I'll go to sleep. It's already night, although it is still light. The sky is bluish-gray and a full moon is shining. Before me there winds a sandy well-worn road, rutted by wagon wheels. I'm already very tired, and I walk slowly. Usually I think about how much longer I'll work, where I'll go afterward, and I almost never come to any conclusion. But why think about it now, when I don't know the situation at the front? Time will tell. Now I long for a bit of rest. And, yet, it seems that there's no greater happiness than weariness after work. Why? I myself don't know. It feels good and pleasant now to be exhausted, and I lazily think how I will soon lie down and fall asleep. On both sides of the road stretch freshly plowed fields; on the right, at the horizon, a yellow line of rye stalks rustles. The moon looks down on me, the same moon that was in Bialystok two years ago. Does she recognize me? Maybe she's confused by my new work clothes? Suddenly it hits me that the moon is very, very old, an old woman. In the past two years she hasn't changed at all, not even her silly smile. But people change so quickly! Here's the little bridge over the narrow brook and here are the first houses. I'm close to my destination.

Saturday the 17th of July [1943]

Work is becoming more unbearable every day. The tractor drivers pick on me because I'm Jewish. They say openly to me that the Jews are the worst people in the world, and that Hitler is right to oppress them. The brigade leader is an anti-Semite in disguise and constantly persecutes me at work. He wants me to measure more land than has been plowed, which would be to his benefit. Yesterday the wooden spout fell into the oil barrel, and we have nothing with which to pour the oil. In the evening I told an assistant that I would be late to work this morning, because I had to get a utensil from the smithy. When I actually arrived at nine o'clock with the spout, he yelled at me again, saying that he'd write a report that I allegedly failed to ask for permission. In the presence of all the tractor drivers, he yelled at me. That gave them the right to throw dirt at me today as I was lying near the wagon. At first I paid no attention, then grew angry, finally left and went into the wagon. They threw dirt inside as well. These insults are choking me: at times my throat constricts with sobs. What have I done to deserve such a fate? I don't know what to do, and I can't tell anyone how I'm suffering. My landlady, the tractor drivers, all the people I have to deal with make trouble for me and nobody defends me. It's a disaster: even in the Soviet Union, anti-Semitism holds sway, twenty-six years after the October Revolution! It is hard, very hard!

Last night I dreamed about my mother; she is on the verge of death. She sat with me in the wagon and the tractor drivers banged on the walls. I awoke later with swollen eyes and a headache.

Sunday the 18th of July [1943]

Sometimes I accuse the tractor drivers of being coarse, crude, cruel. Yes, that's all true. But is it not possible to find the reasons that cause it? Is it really their fault? How could they be polite and good-natured when their lives are so hard and cruel? How can they be educated, since the majority have no opportunity for education? Yesterday something happened that gave me a lot to think about. One of the tractor drivers went to the nearby field for a lever and other tools, and didn't return for a long time. Later the cook, who drove by, found him on the road in a faint. He had battered and bruised his face, which had become ulcerated. She brought him on the wagon, where he regained consciousness. The entire day he lay under the wagon, the only shade there was, with a headache. When the brigade leader arrived, he took him to Karakulino. They arrived at the clinic late, and the doctor was no longer there.

Today he was at work as usual. I thought about it: how many days and weeks would I, or some other "big-city intellectual," have been sick in bed and taken medicine? And he—nothing. He does as much physically hard labor as before. When the tractors are operating, they work twelve hours and more on a shift. Is his life, the life of a sixteen-year-old boy, easy? He is undoubtedly the only bread-winner in the family, and this isn't his first year of work. He has completed only the third grade. What has life given him? Hard work, enough bread and potatoes to eat. And curse words aplenty, tobacco, ragged, filthy clothes. When I consider these circumstances, I forgive them everything. Forgive them even for persecuting me as a Jew. Is it their fault that the people have been indoctrinated with the idea that Jews are the cause of their poverty? It is because of the blind ignorance, the obscurantism, and poverty of the people that they are so depressed and embittered. I'm more and more convinced of how complicated life is and how false was the way I imagined it in my fantasy. Only now do I begin to recognize it.

Monday the 19th of July [1943]

Yesterday they brought us nothing for dinner and supper, and we all went around hungry. We found some berries and ate them right away. One of the tractor drivers brought potatoes from the village, and we made a fire and cooked them. Afterward we picked peas from a nearby field. We completed the shift of 43 hectares, and we're moving the wagon again. One tractor and the barrels of kerosene are already standing in the new location. And the wagon is still in the old place, because we did not manage to move it. It started to rain, and I arrived in the wagon. All wet, I put on my vest and fell asleep. I've gotten used to sleeping in the wagon and it's not really so bad. Everything I have on is wet and it's very cold. Now I have gotten up and my pants are still wet. I think about only one thing—not getting sick!

Thursday the 22nd of July [1943]

And so I wallow in the dirt. The atmosphere all around is just as depressing as before. But I have pledged my word—hold out! At the children's home everybody advises me: quit work! Free yourself somehow! I told them I want to complete a month. What will happen after that, we'll see. Rebecca Izraelevna is very interested in where I'll be going and has even asked her son about the Moscow institutes. On the seventeenth, Tanya arrived from Izhevsk for a vacation. She says that she feels bad here and would like to find work. There's nothing new at the children's home. They say that the director is very strict lately, and not a day goes by without a scene.

Saturday the 24th of July [1943]

Yesterday I was in Karakulino all day at the children's home, because I was called to a meeting of the Raikom of the Komsomol. I've been appointed the *Komsorg* [Komsomol organizer] in Maragino. Last night I slept at the children's home from eleven o'clock until four this morning, when I returned to work. I never enjoyed five hours' sleep as much as I did today. I was clean and slept in a clean bed. What a great luxury! I don't even feel tired now, although I walked 14 kilometers. I feel good and fresh. Tomorrow I have to go to Karakulino again with the accounts for the MTS.

Monday the 26th of July [1943]

It's cloudy and it is hard to tell what time it is. Yesterday I was in Karakulino. Tanya is not working. Everyone advises me to quit work because it is so hard, but I don't want to! Why should I listen to the advice of the "refined intellectuals" who are not used to hard physical labor and difficult conditions? Tanya feels weak. Why does she need to work, since she can expect help from Samuil Markovich? I want to work in order to secure a financial base for my studies. I can endure cold, wetness, curse words, fatigue, and dirt—anything in order to achieve my goal, which I hold sacred!

Yesterday it rained and the ground is wet. My hemp shoes with their cloth uppers and my trousers are all wet. I have to put up with that, too. Finally I'm rid of my old brigade leader, who had gotten under my skin. What the new one will be like—we'll soon find out. Yesterday Vera accompanied me for quite a long distance. She feels bad in the children's home, she has no kindred spirit, she was almost in tears. Sometimes I wonder: Why do the kids treat her like that? True, she is very much an individualist, but she can form attachments. She helps me a lot, for example, for which I am very grateful!

Tuesday the 27th of July [1943]

Yesterday and today we've had very bad weather. There is rain, thunder, and lightning. When I left the fields yesterday evening, it looked like rain. How terrifying is a storm in the open fields! I walk on the road between the fields, hurrying in order to avoid the rain. On the horizon, in every direction heavy black clouds gather, and it's as dark as night. Only in my little corner is it still light. But even here a cloud is fast approaching. Soon there will be a storm. An angry wind howls in the fields. The grass trembles and bends to the ground. Now lightning cuts across the sky and it becomes light for a second and then—dark again. Thunder crashes and its echo can be heard from the nearby valley. Faster, faster home! There are still 3 kilometers to the village. How can I get there safely? I run, and the wind whips me in the face, tears the kerchief from my head, billowing the bottom of my sweater. The first drops start to fall. At first gradually, then faster and faster. I'm already close to the village, but the water drips down on my face, and my sweater gets heavy and waterlogged. When I reach my destination I am already all wet.

Today I went out to the fields and came back because of the rain. Now it's not raining, but it's very humid and we can expect rain again. So I am staying home. I'll probably go to the fields later.

Sunday the 1st of August [1943]

I've been in the children's home for three days already. My foot is sore and I can hardly walk. Now it's a little better and I plan to go back to work in the village. The work has me worried. Nobody is replacing me, and the fuel has been left unattended. Generally, I am eager to get back to the fields. At the children's home it's good to be a guest, but not to live there all the time. Second, it would be a shame to lose the workdays; I have to work to earn bread!

Monday the 2nd of August [1943]

Yesterday I went to work with my bad foot. When I came to the village, I wanted to ask for a horse and wagon. But when I got to the paddock, I found no one there. I had to go on foot. I barely managed to get there, because the sore on my foot kept bothering me. I got to the fields when it was already dark, and I didn't find the brigade leader. In fact, there are now two brigade leaders, along with tractor drivers from the Third and Eleventh Labor Detachments, which have been sent to assist us. They are working, and we are not.

Today the brigade leader arrived. Perhaps we will work today. He's going to Karakulino again. Altogether he's a very careless person. Oh, my shlimazel, my ne'er-do-well? Where are you going?

Wednesday the 4th of August [1943]

My wagon is now a lot more jolly and crowded. I'm very glad about the crowding. The brigade leader of the Third Detachment is a very nice person. His tractor drivers are draftees, who will be going into the army in the autumn. They are better than our tractor drivers. Since they've been here, I feel a lot better. The woman who pays them, Katya, is also a nice woman. They feed us not too badly: three times a day—meat soups, noodles and potatoes! That's actually what drove them to the work as well. There is just one problem: before there was no bread at all, so yesterday they brought fine-looking bread, but bitter! Because the fields were overgrown with bitter weeds. We ate very little of it. But I wasn't hungry, because you can eat as much soup as you want.

Yesterday and today my foot feels better. The only problem is that the weather has been very bad. There's an angry, cold wind blowing. The times when my foot hurts I can't go to the village, so I sleep in the wagon.

Today it was very cold. I lay with Katya on the plank cot and we warmed each other. I'm not wearing socks and I've wrapped my foot in a sack that I found here. In my "office" there's a door and it's warmer, so six tractor drivers came in and lay down on the ground. Sometimes it hurts me that I'm so cut off from the common people, which is in fact the class from which I come. I look at the peasant boys, observe how they go around dirty, in tatters, how they work, how they eat, and I'm reminded of excerpts from films that show workers in tsarist Russia. Actually, the tractor drivers are workers, not peasants. Yesterday evening they sang together. It wasn't singing, but rather a wolflike howling, echoing the wolflike howling of the wind, which nearly blew the wagon away. Again I reflect on their lives: life is very hard but they are used to it and don't complain. Sometimes I think: my life is not easy, because it's harder than Shura Zlatina's, who goes on trips to Sarapul, or to Kazan. Harder, too, than Tanya's, who is working as a Pioneer leader at the children's home! But what do my hardships mean compared to those of the tractor drivers? Even now, when we share the same fate, suffer equally from cold and filth, I have it better, since, in addition, they have to do hard physical labor. Moreover, this is a temporary job for me—and for them, their daily bread.

Saturday the 7th of August [1943]

Living together with the common people, sleeping on the ground on a sheepskin, dressed in dirty trousers, in hemp shoes wrapped in linen, all in all, living like the simple peasant folk, I want to wholly adapt to them, become closer friends with the peasant daughters, in order to understand their lives, know the air they breathe. Unfortunately, I haven't succeeded. Their needs can in no way satisfy me—on the contrary. It would seem that externally I've already adapted—we eat together from the same bowl, scooping honey with a spoon, crumbling bread into the milk. I've even thrown out the pure, literary words from my vocabulary and replaced them with "short and sweet" [a euphemism for obscenities], and so on. But I can compromise no further. I can't join in their gossip, nor do I want to run singing and dancing through the village in the evening, chasing boys. Yesterday, sixty wounded Red Army men from the hospital in Sarapul came here to work. From every corner of the village girls arrived dressed up in white kerchiefs and white dresses in floral patterns. All night long I heard the accordion playing, heard singing, dancing, and laughter. This is the first time I've encountered village entertainment.

Every day I learn more and more about the poverty of the people. Today all the young men born in 1926 were called up for the draft. From our detachment and from the Third, five tractor drivers were taken. Two of them don't even have parents or friends, don't own a clean shirt on their backs, no intact pair of pants to wear before the draft board. The brigade leader of the Third Detachment, a very nice person, gave one of them some money to get a haircut and even lent him a pair of his old pants. I shudder when I think about it: the tractor drivers worked so hard and only for their food. The collective farm seldom gives them the bread that they have earned! I'm reminded of the old revolutionary folk song:

> And you plow and you sow
> And you feed and you sew,
> And you hammer and you spin,
> Tell me, my people, what do you earn?[*]

Sunday the 8th of August [1943]

I don't know why, but it seems to me that life is senseless. I look around me: human beings, representatives of the highest

[*] In fact not a folk song, but a translation by the Yiddish writer Chaim Zhitlowski (1865–1943) of a poem by Georg Herwegh (1817–1875), German poet and hero of the 1848 revolution.

form of life, go about the earth, curse each other, exhaust themselves in order to stuff their bellies. Each one tries to grab the food
from the other's mouth so he can have it for himself, to satisfy his
guts and appease the instinct known as "hunger." As in the city,
people in the villages steal, take bribes and graft. They go to work
unwillingly, as if under the lash. They work any old way. That's why
the bread is full of bitter weeds and is not fit to be eaten. (For two
weeks now we have been eating bitter bread; it's impossible to
swallow more than 100 grams a day of it.) Where is the "merry,
happy collective-farm life"? People make it to sixty or seventy and
then they die. Their children start the same old story all over again.
For what? What is the sense of this comedy, or tragicomedy? Yes, I
do like to study, and to know and understand everything. But what
will come of it? Actually, I do everything to make life better and
more comfortable for myself. An engineer earns more than a
teacher, so I chose that specialty. I, too, silently dream of "quiet
happiness," of a full, interesting life. That happiness may or may
not come, but the day will come when I will die. I won't even be
able to answer the questions: Why have I lived, and what have I
done with my life?

Monday the 9th of August [1943]

Sometimes my soul is torn by conflicting feelings, and a
struggle rages within me. Getting to know the life of the people, I
became acquainted with a world that I hadn't known till now. It
seems to me that this is the authentic life that I did not experience
before. It seems that school, the children's home, all of that is not
important; it is artificial and not typical. There you can't draw on
the folk wisdom that sprouts up from the people, which I remember from my childhood and is again revealed to me now. The
brigade leader of the Third Detachment is a typical representative
of the people, a jolly worker from the city who has migrated to the
country. He bubbles with jokes and anecdotes. He's not a bad
actor, a comedian. It's interesting to chat with him. The tractor

drivers are basically not a bad bunch, and sometimes I regret that I'm not like them. Yesterday they invited me to an evening in their village, Klestovo. I wanted to go in order to acquaint myself with their amusements, to enrich my impressions of their lives. But I didn't go because I could foresee how uncomfortable I would feel among them. I know that my work will be finished soon, in about a month. I'll go off to study and I'll slip into a completely different environment. I regret that my connection with the folk is ending so quickly. I bring to mind, and begin to understand, those back-to-the-land people who traded in urban polish and culture for "the peasant smock." Only now do I sense the meaning of "Tolstoyism," the substance of the theory of "simplicity."

Tuesday the 10th of August [1943]

Last night I went over to Karakulino. Today Genya is supposed to arrive from Moscow. She is coming just for a rest. Then she will return to the capital—or maybe she'll change her itinerary? The question interests me greatly. How will our meeting go? Our encounter? Her letters until now have been few and far between.

Thursday the 26th of August [1943]

Lately, when really important things happen, I don't even have the time to write them down. Genya has been with us for more than two weeks. She is taking a rest after a year of student life. Our relations are cordial and friendly. She is also very close to Tanya, who envies her a lot.

Recently I've been ill, with a fever, dysentery, and total exhaustion. I've already stopped working, and after much effort and spent energy (which I recently discovered I possessed), and with the help of Imzhanov, the secretary of the District Party Committee—who has been especially kind to me—I brought fifteen puds of rye to the children's home over a period of two days!!! Understandably, there's not a single person who does not envy me. Rye now costs 500 rubles a pud and flour 1,000 rubles. I'm proud of my work, which I found by myself and settled into, though everyone predicted that it would be hard.

Now I have a lot of problems with the rye: some of it has to be washed, because it contains bitter weeds, then dried and ground. All of that involves great difficulties. Some of the rye will have to be sold, since I simply won't be able to turn it into flour.

I haven't yet written down the most important thing of all. I received an announcement from the Bauman Technical Institute in Moscow that I've been accepted into the entering class! I need to be there on the tenth of September! I am very pleased. Moscow! My dream has come true! To receive a permit to travel there I have to go to Izhevsk. There's little time left, and I'm afraid that I'll be too late. Our director is now in Sarapul, and I must wait until he comes back. In the meantime I have to deal with the rye myself. I'm in a good mood: one of self-satisfaction and expectation of happiness!

Sunday the 5th of September [1943]

I've been on the road for seven days now. In the evening of the twenty-ninth, I took the steamer to Izhevsk to get the permit to travel to Moscow. Now I am going back to Karakulino. I received the permit, became familiar with modern means of communication, breathed the city air that I had longed for so much. Only one thing saddened my first excursion: at the market a thief cut up my new green summer coat! By my foreign appearance he thought I had a lot of money in my pocket, so he decided to cut it out. Naturally he found nothing, though, as a matter of fact, there was money in my handbag. But he ruined my coat!

Now there's a new problem: this is the second day I've been sitting in Sarapul waiting for a steamer. I used up all my food quite a while ago. I've already spent 500 rubles after selling a pud of rye for 600 rubles, and have no money left. For the time being I've been sleeping and eating in the Sarapul children's home. The food here is worse than at our place, but what can I do?

The most important thing is that I have little time left and a lot to do. Today is the fifth of September and I have to be in Moscow on the tenth. I'll be in my dormitory no sooner than the seventh. I'll have to wash, dry, and iron my clothes, wash and dry the rye to cook, grind, and sell, and buy butter and honey for myself. When will I manage to do it all? My trip to Moscow involves quite a lot of baggage and a lot of difficulties. Still, I am happy! My entire dream is coming true! I want to get there as fast as possible. As fast as possible to the heart of the Union!

Friday the 10th of September [1943]

I sit in Karakulino on pins and needles. My clothes are all packed. I just have to sell the flour. The girls washed and dried all the rye. The day that I arrived I ground it at the steam mill. The hardest thing now is selling it. Today I stood in the market for half a day and sold nothing. My last hope is Sunday, when there will be a market. Then I'll sell it for whatever I can get. I've been offered 1,100 rubles for a pud, but I've been told that last Sunday the price was 1,400 rubles. I have 11.5 puds of flour. I am very, very rich!

Wednesday the 22nd of September [1943]

My hoped-for dream has come true! I've torn myself away from remote, muddy Karakulino, where I spent two years. Now I am in Moscow! The seventeenth of September, four years to the day after Molotov ordered the crossing of the Polish frontier to free Western White Russia from German occupation,[*] four years after my first enthusiasm, my new enthusiasm begins. On the seventeenth, at ten in the morning, I saw the capital for the first time. Now a new life is beginning for me: I am a student at Moscow's

[*] On September 17, 1939, Soviet forces invaded Poland, in keeping with the Molotov-Ribbentrop pact, whereby Poland was to be divided between Germany and the Soviet Union. The annexed regions, rebaptized Western White Russia (Belarus) and Western Ukraine, were "liberated" from Polish (not German) rule.

Bauman Technical Institute called the Ernst Bauman Institute. I'll live in a splendid room with four other female students. I have the opportunity to visit the best theaters, movies, museums, cultural monuments. The gates of knowledge and culture have opened for me! I am no longer the poor inmate of a children's home; I am very rich! I brought with me 1.5 puds of flour, 2.5 kilos of melted butter, 3 kilos of honey, 4 kilos of onions, and 1 kilo of fine meal (which now goes for 600 rubles). I have 4,500 rubles in my pocket, not counting the money I paid for the trip here.

"Tempora mutantur nos et mutamur in illis." "The times are changing and we are changing with them," so goes the Latin proverb! Now I have only to buy some clothes so I can be decently dressed, because I still look like a beggar. I have every reason to be proud of my work, which has provided me with a whole year of studies. Nobody advised me to go to work, but when I left Karakulino, everyone envied me. Oh, where is my good mother? Why shouldn't she be able to enjoy my success?

Thursday the 23rd of September [1943]

I'm sitting in the room of my communal residence. The autumn rain beats against the windowpanes. The room is clean and pleasant. Valya, a third-year student, is resting after her work. Lilka is reading a book. I look around. Every year I'm making progress: in the room there's electricity, central heating, a radio! When did I ever live in such luxury? Gradually I've become familiar with the streetcar system, with the card system, with meal regulations in restaurants. I can't wait for the school year to start. I want to work, to study. And I so much want to live! I'm in my nineteenth year, and I am full of vigor. I hold my head high!

The days fly by in Moscow. I spend whole days riding the streetcar from the institute to our communal apartment, to dining halls and food depots. My money is running out like water; my food supplies—honey and butter—are also running out, because there are three of us eating. The most important thing is that classes haven't yet begun. Who knows if they'll start on the first of October? They have tried to mobilize me for work somewhere, but so far nothing has come of it. Meanwhile, my heart is empty. I feel so lonley now! In my apartment building there are many students, but I don't know them yet. Many of them are married; they live in family units, as adults, each with his own work and worries.

Every day I go to see Manya Liberman, who was, like me, a student in the Karakulino school. Until recently I lived with her. She's always busy with her own affairs, so we aren't close friends. Her mother, a typical Jewish mama, idolizes her daughter, gives her hugs and kisses. Whenever I witness such demonstrations of affection, my heart cries inside. There is no one who loves me. Nobody worries about me, thinks about me. I'm all alone in a city of five million people. People are busy with their own lives. I'm already used to that. They are interested in their homes, food, clothes. Even Lilka and Valya are more interested in my honey and butter than in me. Such is the law of nature. Now I long for a close friend! For my mother! Materially, I'm taken care of for now. For the time being, I cannot complain. Psychologically, I am lonely. Soon Genya will be arriving. We'll have a chance to grow close. I want the school year to begin already. The more work, the better!

From the front there's now a lot of encouraging news: Every day the capital salutes the heroic Red Army—in Kharkov, Poltava, Smolensk! The enemy is already running back! Soon the war will end in our victory! Maybe I'll soon be able to go home. See my dear parents, my little sister and brother?

Now I hear salvos. That is the salute to the heroic liberators of Smolensk. Twenty artillery salvos from 224 cannon. Red, green, yellow fireworks flash across the dark red sky. A sign of hope!

Sunday the 26th of September [1943]

Today I did something that no one can forgive me for: I spent 90 rubles on snacks. In such hard times! At the market I saw apples. The last time I ate an apple was in Bialystok, at the end of the summer of 1940. When I saw them now, my heart couldn't resist. I ate four apples. For that much money I could have bought 4 kilos of potatoes and eaten for an entire week, aside from the midday meal in the student dining hall. But you can't always behave rationally.

Wednesday the 29th of September [1943]

A few days ago Genya arrived. I was very happy to see her. I feel lonely most of the time. But she is my closest friend!

I've broken off with everything having to do with the Karakulino children's home, with the two years that I lived there. Now I find myself in quite a different environment—one of young intellectuals, the student body, which I'm just starting to get to know. Genya has introduced me to her girlfriends, students at the university. They invite me to their rooms for conversation, reading, and so forth. I'm starting to feel that my feet are firmly planted on the ground.

Wednesday the 6th of October [1943]

I am starting to lead a normal student life. I get up at six in the morning, clean up, wash up and eat breakfast—I still have some butter and sugar! At eight o'clock I go off to the institute, where I stay till two thirty. From the institute I go to the restaurant, where I eat the midday meal and also supper. With that and 200 grams of bread I am satisfied! I go back to the reading room of the institute, where I find the appropriate literature for my courses, as well as newspapers, and the like. At eight in the evening I return to our dormitory, have some more bread and butter, sometimes with herring and onions that I saved from the midday meal. I read a book until eleven o'clock, and then go to sleep. The days pass normally. I am pleased with the curriculum. True, the work looks like it will not be easy, especially technical drawing and theoretical mechanics. I hope that I'll learn it. My goal now is to better, and more fundamentally master the subject matter, so that I turn out to be a good engineer. Sometimes I dream that as a young engineer I'll go back home to my dear parents, who have already mourned for me! My beloved mother will be glowing with happiness! So many of her hopes were placed on me. That's why I must attain my goal. Study with persistence and penetrate the science!

Although I've been in Moscow for almost three weeks, I don't yet know the city well. I simply don't have the time to visit the city. It's not so easy to do for now. On Sunday I was at the theater with Misha, who also came here from Karakulino, and we saw Korneichuk's *Front*. Misha comes here quite often, but I'm quite indifferent to him.

Sunday the 10th of October [1943]

I'm overcome with a general feeling of dissatisfaction. I've been a student for ten days. Every day I go to the institute, listen to the lectures, attend the seminars and the labs. But afterward I do nothing else. Keeping house takes up the whole time, the time intended for studying. After the midday meal I go to our dormitory, or to the market. In the afternoon I have to clean, prepare supper, wash, iron, and so on. The day passes. In the evening and even during the day, it's impossible to work in our room, so I have to travel to the reading room at the institute. I feel that my time is dribbling away on silly trifles, which nevertheless have to be carried out. I must tear myself away from cooking (a good thing there's something to cook), mending, sewing, washing, ironing. Starting tomorrow I'll remain at the institute every day so I can study rigorously.

Tuesday the 12th of October [1943]

Today there are no lectures in our class. We've all been sent to work on the third line of the metro at Izmailovo station. We worked for eight hours. We're supposed to work tomorrow and the day after tomorrow as well. The metro station has to be finished by the seventh of November, [anniversary of the Revolution], so all students have been mobilized. I come home from work exhausted, yet the rewards are great—moral satisfaction! How pleasant it will be to stroll in this station, ride on the underground train, knowing that I took part in its construction.

The only problem is that we have interrupted our studies, in which I haven't yet immersed myself as I should. In general I have to consider my plans, examine myself: the entire time in Karakulino I strove to get out of there as fast as possible, to pursue higher education in Moscow so that I could study seriously, take in the cultural life. Now I have reached my goal: I am in Moscow, I study at an institute. And what's more, I don't belong to the category of impoverished students who live a hungry life. That is, I live in good circumstances, relatively, by wartime standards, of course! But, as if for spite, I do not study. The first twelve days I've just wandered around. Naturally, I won't let that happen any longer. I must work conscientiously, study rigorously. The most important thing is not to forget my goal, not lose myself in a sea of trivial daily chores, in my petty housekeeping. I must complete the first term with excellent grades, though I know that's very hard to do. But—only those who believe are victorious!

Monday the 25th of October [1943]

Almost a month of study has gone by. I feel as if I've lost track of my studies and now must catch up. There is altogether a great deal of work, and I'm afraid that I have little to show for it. In general, I notice that others study more effectively and conscientiously. I'm actually ashamed of myself, and I'm making every effort. Many others face such difficulties. For example, Olga

Palabugina, who also came from Karakulino to study at the [Bauman] Energy Institute, has decided to go back home. Yesterday, I expended much energy in trying to talk her out of this step. I still don't know what she finally decided to do. It's very significant that, practically every evening in our dormitory, there's no longer any electricity. It goes on only after midnight, when everybody is asleep. I waste plenty of time each day in the dining hall for the midday meal. To continue in our studies, there's a bare minimum that we must accomplish. I must show them that I cannot go back—that I have no home! I must master the science!

Thursday the 4th of November [1943]

Only now do I begin to understand what is meant by an independent life. I have a sense of adult self-sufficiency. Now there are no more Mama and Papa, who for sixteen years enveloped me in their warm, soft wings. Now there are not even Fanny Pavlovna and Samuil Markovich, whose obligation it was to bear the burden of financial concern. I have to think of everything, foresee everything. If I don't take my shoes to the shoemaker in time—and I have to do that soon!—I'll remain without shoes and nobody will give me another pair! If I don't make an effort to get liquor at the warehouse, my ration card will expire and I'll lose the 300 rubles I could earn at the market! If I don't manage (because the electricity is on only for a limited time now) to cook potatoes for myself, I am hungry all day long! The smallest trifles, petty daily cares, take so much time and are hard to manage.

There remains little time for study, and that's why we—all the students—are falling behind in technical drawing. That can end very badly: will we get scholarships? There is much energy in my struggle for existence. I brace myself, because sometimes my morale is low. I long for a normal life, for a home, for a soul mate. Meanwhile, I envy those who do have a home. But I know all too well that, for me, there no longer exists such a thing. The wound is too painful and too old for me to spend time reminiscing. The first year away from home . . . [several words missing]. Now my heart is hardened and doesn't feel what is called love. Will this young, warm, girlish heart wither away?

Life is cruel and difficult. There is a lot of work and I can't manage to do what needs to be done. All the same, I have to waste at least one and a half to two hours a day in order to eat the main meal in the dining hall and then feel hungry the rest of the day, because there's no place to cook my potatoes and flour. Still, I have to waste time figuring out when there'll be food at the depot, when they're distributing wine. Today I got a liter of port and sold it right away at a profit of 300 rubles. Still, I must go to the bathhouse and wait in line all day, then wash, press, mend. Yes, I'm engulfed in a fog of petty chores, working fast, studying. And I don't even have the time to make sense of my situation, to reexamine it. I'm always in a hurry, always in harness like the ox to the plow. As it turns out, student life in Moscow bears no resemblance to what I had imagined.

In the one and a half months that I have been here, I've only been once to the theater and twice to the movies. And twice to films at the institute. I've hardly seen Moscow at all. I only know the way from the communal apartment to the Institute, the trip I take every day. I get up at six thirty, wash, comb my hair, and travel to the dining hall. But not always! Sometimes I make do with just some bread. The institute is across the street from the dining hall. At two thirty, classes are over. So I go to the dining hall again, which takes up another two hours every day and gives you the illusion of being full. Then I go to the library at the institute, and then to the dorm room to sleep. So it goes, day in, day out. Sunday is given over to the drawing class or taking care of domestic needs. So the days go by, life's precious hours and minutes.

Today I went to the Union of Polish Patriots to ask for financial aid and some clothes. There I found many Jews from Lvov, Warsaw, Vilna, even Bialystok. Several girls are studying at the drama school of the Yiddish Theater. From them I learned the fate of Benny Weiner (we were students together at the Yiddish Gymnazium in Bialystok). It appears that he was arrested in 1940 [by the soviet authorities] after he had been a student for several months. The reason for his arrest is unknown. What a fate! I wrote down the address of their student housing. I once dreamed about the drama school, but now the question is much less relevant. But I absolutely must make some connection with Yiddish culture! They told me that Mikhoels[*] will soon be arriving from America. Maybe it will be possible to set up a Yiddish Cultural Center. Maybe I'd find something there that's familiar, intimate? I've already forgotten some of my Yiddish, along with my Polish, German, Latin—all languages that I once knew. What have I learned? Very little, except perhaps a bit of practical life.

Monday the 8th of November [1943]

Yesterday and today are holidays: the twenty-sixth anniversary of the October Revolution. There are no classes at the institute now, and nobody is working anywhere. The people are celebrating the great holiday. And I? Valya has gone off to a Moscow friend of hers and Lilka to her aunt for the holiday. Zina and Xenia are preparing for a drinking party that their group is organizing. What should I do? Yesterday, feeling lonely, I had an idea: I should go to Rebecca Izraelevna's; maybe she's already arrived from Karakulino. After dragging myself for an hour and a half on the streetcar, I finally arrived at my destination, but, as it turned out, the room was locked. Rebecca Izraelevna is not there yet, has not yet arrived. Where should I go now? An idea occurs to me: go visit Manya Liberman, so as not to remain so alone! Again a half hour's ride, and again nobody is home. Like a drunkard I stagger to the streetcar and get out near the movie theater. Maybe a film will ease my pain. But there are so many people in the ticket line that, at four o'clock, there's no hope of getting in. I have to go back home. Embittered, lonely, abandoned by everyone, I make it to our communal room. Soon it will be dark. We have no electricity here, so what should I do? How do I get rid of my thoughts? But suddenly—

[*] Solomon Mikhoels (1890–1948) was the director of the Moscow State Yiddish Theater, who in 1943 was sent on a good-will mission to America. Suspected of Jewish nationalism, Mikhoels was murdered in 1948 on Stalin's orders.

a miracle! Lilka has arrived with tickets to the opera. They are play-ing *Eugene Onegin.*[*] Faster, faster, it's getting late! Last night I got home at midnight. I liked the opera a lot and enjoyed myself greatly. A simple coincidence saved the day.

Wednesday the 10th of November [1943]

The days are turning gray. It's winter already. The Moscow streets were covered with wet snow, which froze in the evening and made the streets slippery. All day long I sat in the library of the institute and did my homework. I've just gotten home. Nobody is home and it's dark, because there is still no electricity. I'm in the reading room of the communal apartment, but I'm very tired and will soon go to sleep. How foolish life is—no happiness, no enjoy-ment, no pleasures. Intense work in poor conditions, daily petty cares, which become tedious but cause bad blood. In addition, the loneliness that chills and hardens your heart. I long for a sincere, warm word, for some hope, for my mother! After two and a half years of life as an orphan, I hope and yearn. I will never, ever have a home, or find a kindred spirit. Why, fate?

Sunday the 21st of November [1943]

I just received a letter from Karakulino. Vera and Shura write that Samuil Markovich will soon be coming to Moscow. It should happen in the next few days. It will be interesting to see what our meeting is like. Before my departure he wasn't overly friendly; there were even small incidents. How will it be now? I'm glad that he's coming—someone I know, after all! An acquain-tance, but unfortunately not a very close one.

It's very pleasant to get a letter from Karakulino, especially from Vera—warm, cordial letters. But on the other hand a deep pain creeps into my heart! Vera and Shura think that I live an interesting

[*]Opera by Tchaikovsky based on Pushkin's play.

life, go to the movies and theater often, belong to circle of cultured people. They think that I've excelled at the institute, that I take part in performances of the drama circle. Vera asks if I'm still writing my short story. And warns me that I absolutely must keep writing, in order to further develop my talent! And I? I haven't picked up a book, not to mention my short story. I have to do my homework, have a lot of work to do on my first set of drawings, and by the fifteenth of December I have to have my second set ready!

Sunday the 28th of November [1943]

At the Union of Polish Patriots, specifically, at the committee for social assistance, I received: low shoes, two jackets, a blouse, a sweater-vest, a shirt, a pair of pants, a pair of woolen socks, and gloves. Naturally, none of them are new; they're worn and used. Nevertheless, it's a fine gift and worth 7,000 to 8,000 rubles! It's possible that I may even get a blanket!

Today I was at Rebecca Izraelevna's. She's already in Moscow. She received me very warmly and at once turned the conversation to the money she owes me for the pud of flour I gave her in Karakulino. I will under no circumstances take money from her! She wants to give me a dress, but I don't want to take it. She brought me letters from the girls in Sarapul. Naturally, all the director's golden promises turned out to be worthless.

Tuesday the 30th of November [1943]

Nineteen years old—today! Why don't I sense my youth in bloom? Moscow of the five million inhabitants has swallowed me into its bowels, has screwed me into its mighty work-engine, and day in, day out I perform the same movements, wake up to the same cares and duties. For three years I had dreamed about the capital, about the brilliance of its cinema, about the theaters, concerts, and balls. I counted the days till I could tear myself away from the remote village, from the suffocating atmosphere of the children's home, and become independent. I attained my goal! Those two [sic] years have been erased from my memory. I'm now independent, but my current life doesn't resemble my dream. I have no regrets and I don't want to go back there. I have made peace with the present and am launching a new struggle for my existence, though it's very hard for me. But I'm faced with the question of my present and my future.

Unfortunately, I am falling behind in technical drawing. I have to study hard in order to get a scholarship! Lately we have had electricity in our room in the evening and at night, so I have to get going on the drawing. On the eleventh of December, we have to finish the first two sheets. By then I'll have to catch up from lagging behind. Five to six hours of sleep is enough for me. The rest belongs to my studies.

I'm already an independent, mature person: I need to get back on track, work out a plan for my studies, because I'm responsible for my actions. I swim all alone in the mighty ocean of life. It's hard for me, but I must overcome the difficulties. "What is difficult is not impossible." I have to work seriously!

Thursday the 9th of December [1943]

My first drawings have been rejected. The chairman of the department sent for me and suggested that I do the work over. Today I was enrolled in a class in India-ink drawing. Sunday one of our teachers will show me how to work with India ink, on the orders of the lecturer, the department chairman. The dean and chairman treat me very well. So I have to show them that I'm worthy of such treatment.

The most important thing for a person is to find a place for himself in life. I slave away, but find no way out. I suffer from hunger. Morning and evening I am always hungry, except for the midday meal in the dining hall at the institute. I still have a little butter and honey, which I keep at Manya Liberman's, but I have no time to pick it up. My flour is also there, but where would I bake it? All my treasures are of no use. My hunger is my own fault! Psychologically, things are no better: my studies at the institute do not satisfy my soul. Sometimes I think about transferring to the university. When will I do it? I'm very lonely. I don't want to call Genya. She didn't even send me greetings on my birthday. I can't go visit Rebecca Izraelevna very often because I don't have the time, and besides, I'm uncomfortable disturbing her. Now she is preoccupied with herself and with her son. I also go very seldom to visit Manya. I've become friendly with Mayke Krugliak, a student in my class. We both have a lot of worries. Sundays she goes to her aunt's for the whole day. But the rest of the week we're both very busy and do our homework together, or go to the dining hall together. We are both dissatisfied, all in all.

Lately I don't even feel like writing my diary anymore.

Monday the 7th of February [1944]

A rather long time has passed. I would certainly have left the institute by now, if that did not involve my housing and bread and food-ration cards. Now I've completed all my exams and passed them. On the exam in analytic geometry I got an "Excellent"! Now I'm preparing my mathematical analysis.

My food ration cards for the entire month, along with all my documents and money, were stolen. I live on what my roommates give me. Things are grim indeed!

Sunday the 14th of May [1944]

It's May again. Once more the fields are turning green, once more the woods are in bloom, everywhere things are blossoming, every blade of grass, every flower! I will soon go mad, because an angry autumn wind is blowing in my soul. A demon sits inside me and tears me to pieces: I arranged to study at the institute. So I left the surroundings with which I had become familiar, and I felt lonely. I started running to the theater. That costs plenty of money, but it brings me a bit of pleasure. The magnificent ballet *Don Quixote* at the Bolshoi, *Comedians* at a branch of the Maly Theater, concerts in the Great Hall of the conservatory. It lulls you into the mist of dreams, of art, of a higher, exalted, festive spirit. Afterward, you begin to feel an emptiness, pain, loneliness! The cruelest punishment for a human being!

I have three acquaintances: Genya, Rebecca Izraelevna, and Manya Liberman. Genya is busy with herself. She cares about her physical appearance, about clothes, about flirting. I doubt if she thinks of me as often as once a month. She cares more about the women with whom she lives because she gets small favors from them. Rebecca Izraelevna is very caring, invites me to her place often, but I know that she has to care for her son. Her concern for me expresses itself in feeding me when I visit. In that sense she reminds me of my Aunt Alte, whom I used to visit every Sabbath and eat *farfl* [noodle] cookies. But my aunt never had a conversation with me, or my brother and sister; that simply did not concern her. Manya is a petty bourgeois, who thinks about how to get married as soon as possible and become a housewife. I envy her, because she has a loving mother!

What should I do with myself and my loneliness?

Saturday the 12th of August [1944]

A sharp pain has pierced my innermost being. Fifteen days have passed since my numerous letters and cards went off to Bialystok with the first mail after the liberation of the city. My letters were the first! That's what the girl at the post office told me. With tense nerves, like tautly-stretched strings, I wait for an answer, for a couple of lines, at least a couple of words from my faraway home. Meanwhile, there reigns an oppressive silence like that in a cemetery, which tugs at my soul. Instead of an answer, sensational articles in the newspaper about the death camp near Lublin, at

Majdanek: electric ovens where, day and night, they burn living and dead victims from Poland, Lithuania, Czechoslovakia, Italy, and France. People are torn to pieces, hacked with axes and knives. Oh, what a horror!

Bialystok burned for five days, set on fire by the enemy before its retreat. The Bialystok ghetto was also set on fire. After all this news, can I still have hope? What should I do with my heart? Three-fourths of it is paralyzed, numb. One-fourth still flutters. My heart-strings vibrate, and sometimes I feel a bit of warmth stirring! A bit of love for those who still exist there. My home—now it is part of Poland.* Are my loved ones still there? I am waiting for an answer. How long will I be able to endure? After so many days, to receive nothing. . . . With every passing day my hope dims. And the pain begins!

Wednesday the 6th of September [1944]

Life makes its own way, swallows up the individual. The pain of waiting has ended with a greater pain: all the many letters that I sent to Bialystok have been returned with the notation that the addressees are absent. The horror is clear: they all perished as martyrs! And I become a sad creature with many sorrows. But my youthful dreams and plans still remain. I'm sentenced to loneliness, but I cannot be alone. I want to live and enjoy life's splendor!

I have already entered the university in the Classics Department of the Faculty of Philology. I wait impatiently for the day when the school year begins. The physical conditions will be worse. The university doesn't yet have a communal dormitory, and I'll have to stay where I am now. Perhaps they'll evict me. Where will I live? I have no idea. For many years I've dreamed of studying at a university. Now I have attained it. I am still working, though I'm somewhat unwell. I'm not living in my room, because it's being renovated. I am waiting for the first of October, when my new fate will take shape.

---

* Unlike most of eastern Poland, which they had occupied in 1939, the Soviets returned Bialystok to Poland at the end of the war.

Monday the 18th of September [1944]

How complicated is the intertwining of joy and sorrow in my life. How many emotions are tearing at my breast! Will I have enough words to capture with precision all that is raging in my soul, boiling in my blood?

I have been in Moscow exactly a year. How have I experienced this year, how have I changed?

A few days ago here in Moscow I came across my dear teacher Mashevitsky and his family. They left Bialystok when the Nazis arrived and went to their family in Moscow. Until now I didn't know that. What a huge role this encounter now plays in my life! I will never forget them, just as I'll never forget my unhappy people. My teacher's son, Yulik Mashevitsky, is also studying in Moscow. He has now become my close friend. From now on we are no longer alone. Both of us—two Jewish youths— will go together through this difficult life. May heaven bless us! May our people still live!

Here is what he wrote to me:

Dear Leykele!

The seventeenth of September is for me one of the happiest days of my life. I have once again found meaning in my spiritual life. Physically I existed, but there was no one close to me who could understand me, who could sympathize with me, experience what I am experiencing.

Now I have found a comrade with whom I can boldly go hand in hand down life's thorny path, with whom I can be proud that I belong to an ancient historic people that has lived through much and also contributed much to human culture, civilization, and development.

I despise my Bialystok friends who are ashamed of their Jewishness. I am writing to you the eighteenth in the evening. I have just come home from work. I feel that I am missing something. Only now I feel how much I love you!

Sunday the 24th of September [1944]

Before my eyes stands his photograph: golden hair, blue eyes that peer at me, passionate thin lips; a buttoned military jacket and shoulder patches with two stars. On the other side, an inscription: "Your Yulik." My Yulik? Mine always. Forever? Could anyone be happier than I? My eyes drink in the face on the photograph. Can you feel it there, among your soldiers, how I follow your movements in my thoughts? Can you feel my stormy heart beating? It's silly to kiss the paper with your photograph, but can you feel it now, how I write and tremble?

Friday the 29th of September [1944]

My youth is full of springtime
My heart has blossomed out
In dreams I hear the sounds of singing
A turtledove-like flute.

Sad autumn's leaves turn golden
They rustle as they fall.
But May is in my blood now
Life's wellspring bubbles forth.

In dreams of love you lull me
Your glance intoxicates.
Oh lover, come with kisses,
And crush my burning heart.

The borders of our ancient stock
Are now spread wide apart,
Enclosing victims of the flames
In camps where they were strewn.

The ashes of the tortured dead
Demand revenge from us.
And so we swear eternal hate
Toward the evil foe.

There's none can separate us now
We're woven of one cloth,
Our Jewish blood flows proud in us
For we have struggled much.

Monday the 23th of October [1944]

Now I believe that I am destined to live a long life, in order
to create, to work, to be of use! That, apparently, is why fate has
saved me from death so often, why it led me, five days before the
war, out of the brown[*] hell, why it gave me the opportunity to cross
the threshold of Moscow University! Now, it has pulled me out of
the cold arms of the Angel of Death, carried me out from under the
wheels of an electric train alive, though wounded. Twenty days ago,
at eight in the morning, unconscious, and with terrible black eyes,
I looked around and frightened my girlfriends. Then I came to, and
felt a strong pain in my left side; blood was dripping from my
mouth—and gushing from my head.

On the same train that had injured me, I was taken to the hospital in Sokolniki. The wounds on my head were stitched, and I was
diagnosed with slight nervous shock, a broken rib, internal bleed-
ing, and an inflammation of the left side. For the first few days I
couldn't move. Then I began to heal. Here I am at home almost
healed. In a few days I'll go ahead with my studies.

My comrades and friends moved me more than anything else: I
learned that I am not alone, that I am loved, that I haven't been forgotten! Despite the hard times, people brought me grapes, apples,
candy, stewed fruit, and butter. I had many visitors, and the care
that surrounded me moved me greatly. What have I done to

[*]Reference to the brownshirts or Nazi Stormtroopers.

deserve it? Now I understand how much responsibility has been placed on me. I will repay it with my work!

Thursday the 26th of October [1944]

I'm returning to health. My head doesn't hurt anymore, I can walk around a bit, even take a stroll. One thing has remained, and apparently will last for a long time: a pain in my chest and on my left side.

I have to make peace with the pain, as the doctor said, because that is a question of time, perhaps even of years. In other words, farewell youthful walk, mobility, playful, careless gestures! Soon I'll be twenty years old, but I'm already an old woman. I make every effort to mask the pain.

I believe that the joy of happiness comes from the fact that it usually happens suddenly and in small doses—just a few drops. Fate has smiled on me and I am happy. I have found a partner in life who is tied to me by my past, my childhood, and my education—all things that I lost so tragically fast, and that I hold in my heart like a shrine. I am no longer alone. I have a friend with whom I can share my hopes and beliefs, my plans and dreams. The most important thing is that I know that he loves me, thinks about me, cares! That makes me feel very rich! But life is so constructed that there must be obstacles, thorns on the path of growing up, because joy and sorrow are true sisters. We know each other well, and yet—very little. In the fantasy of each of us, there's a false picture drawn from the old prewar photograph, because we hardly knew each other then. There was a gap of age and milieu. Our illusions are based on the old external luster that lost its beauty long ago. Four years of war have also changed a lot of things. Now, once more we live in different circumstances, which prevent us from becoming close. First of all, the accidental obstacles, like my illness and his departure for the army, although he'll soon return.

My circumstances as a student are difficult; he is a lieutenant in the army, studying to be a military interpreter, whose living conditions are also far from satisfactory. All of this is the cause of our distance. Both of us have limited opportunities, and we can't do anything about it. He is very busy and can only see me rarely—only one evening a week, especially now when I'm still not studying. I know that in less than a month he will depart for the front. I'll be losing him for who knows how long—perhaps forever. I shudder at the thought. And yet, we have our obligations to society and to the nation!

Friday the 27th of October [1944]

I'm gradually returning to health, which makes me very happy! The everyday woes of economic hardship are beginning. I don't have a kopeck to my name—but rather, large debts. There are still five days till the end of the month, and my ration cards have long been used up. They cut everything out for meals at the hospital! In the meantime, I'm being fed by my close friend from the institute, Mayke Krugliak, who, all along, has shown how concerned she is about me. But I have to repay her; she herself has very limited resources.

In addition, the housing question is very strained. For the time being I'm still living in the institute dormitory. Sooner or later I'll be expelled from here, and I have nowhere to go. No one knows me yet at the university; because of my illness I haven't yet attended classes.

My fate is to be an eternal wanderer and beggar, a donkey in the heavy harness of life. How little joy, how much grief!

Yulik comes and tells about his stressful work, about the studies that swallow him up. Now I see how little he belongs to me, or even to himself!

When he comes to see me, we are never alone. We're always together with my roommates, who feel inconvenienced by his presence, and sometimes they subtly let me sense it. But he doesn't understand, I don't know why. Maybe he doesn't understand the conditions of communal living, because he has his own room at his friends' place. This bothers me a lot, and consequently I have to do some double-edged play acting: for him, so he won't feel my pain, and for them, to lessen their dissatisfaction!

Saturday the 28th of October [1944]

Today I went to the university for the first time. But I haven't attended any classes yet.

Saturday the 4th of November [1944]

I've been going to classes for a week. Every day I get up at seven in the morning, because classes start at nine. I come home every day at six or seven o'clock in the evening. There is plenty of work, if I want to study properly. It's true that I attend classes in all my subjects, go to all the lectures, prepare my homework in German. After the holiday I'll go often to the library, to get to know the readings. Here it's all very interesting! It requires a lot of time and the right conditions. Despite the fact that, as usual, my circumstances are not brilliant—the constant lack of money!—I must still bear my goal in mind and study seriously: I have a lot to learn! Merely wasting time makes no sense!

Sunday the 5th of November [1944]

I'm in an easy, happy mood. All evening long I chatted about everything and nothing, as usual. Yulik came and left soon afterward. I chatted with Devik, Mayke's old schoolmate, quite an interesting young man!

The holiday is coming soon—the twenty-seventh anniversary of the October Revolution. We're preparing to celebrate it in our room.

My feelings for Yulik have cooled off a bit. I see him for a few minutes once a week. Now we have nothing to talk about since, in addition to the great difference in our personalities, we also have no interests in common. He treats me well, thinks highly of me, but we seldom see each other. I want to talk to him about everything, but I don't know how to find the right approach. Will he be able to understand me? Will I be able to explain things to him?

Monday the 6th of November [1944]

Anger, despair, anxiety, humiliation!

Yulik promised to come over to discuss how we'd celebrate the holiday, and he didn't come. Tomorrow is the holiday! I arranged a modest party in the room, and all the preparations are fully under way. Tomorrow night we will celebrate. Everyone knows that he's coming. But does he? Why didn't he come? Is the reason financial? Was it uncomfortable for him to come over without bringing wine or something else? Why does he keep silent? Why is he playacting, and playacting badly?

We collected some money, and at the market we bought potatoes, beets, and other vegetables, oil, and beans; and there is wine, too. Tomorrow we may even get sweets at the store. It all looks like it will be very good. But I am nervous and even more upset, and very angry. At whom? At him? Actually, I ought to be angry with him. Why does he cause me so much pain? Isn't he capable of behaving differently? I believe he is, but he doesn't understand me. Why? Does he think too little about me? I am angry at myself. Why can't I react calmly? Why must I get upset and nervous? Why am I such a slave to my own foolish heart?

Wednesday the 8th of November [1944]

Last night came off better than might have been expected. Our table was well prepared, the atmosphere was wonderful. In the middle of the party, Genya and Lyonya arrived. Everything was fine, as before. Then she started to flirt with Yulik, so that everyone in the room couldn't help but notice. He responded warmly to her overtures, and that understandably affected my mood. True, Devik, Mayke's friend, was following me with his eyes the entire time. He is a chess master, first class, and has won matches with Botvinnik and Liliental. I kept filling his glass with wine, and gradually he became drunk. Naturally, none of this escaped Yulik. Maybe he was paying me back for that. When he said good-bye, he pressed my hand warmly and for a long time. I recall with what anger and how badly he spoke about her when I was lying in the hospital. It may be that he thinks more highly of me than of her. How should I behave? Pretend not to have noticed? Where is my pride? I even hinted to him that our rare visits, going to the theater—he takes me quite often!—our formal conversations, do not satisfy me. I long to be with him more often! We see each other so seldom.

Thursday the 9th of November [1944]

It's now seven weeks since my accident. A drop of happiness, thankfulness to fate—I'm not one of those who can easily be broken. The electric railway did not break me, merely chained me to my bed for a month. Now I am completely mended. My road is still long and open. I want to study and I will! With all of my being, all of my soul. I know that the university will swallow me up. I will return to work!

Monday the 13th of November [1944]

There was a quiet knock on our door and Yulik appeared! He invited me, along with his family, to his place to meet a partisan from Bialystok. We went there, but it turned out that no one had yet arrived. We spent a pleasant evening at a well-prepared table and had a friendly conversation. His family invited me to visit them often. My current relationship with Yulik is now more formal. In a month he must return to the front. He has a lot of work now, and much depends on his success in this work. He has to be very careful. I am grateful to him, because he's very concerned about me and my future! I have to leave the dormitory at the institute, and I haven't yet gotten any housing at the university.

Tuesday the 28th of November [1944]

Unpleasantness and stress at the Bauman Institute, then work. The news of the death of my parents, my sister and brother, the whole family. The terrible, miserable accident with the train. What a horrible year! Tomorrow is my birthday. What will life be like at twenty? I'm already at the university. This coming year will be the happiest of my life! I have attained my goal, after all. Broad horizons have opened up for me, interesting, intense work. I'm very pleased. But, now it's evening and I'm psychologically exhausted. Why? Why do I work so hard, suffer from hunger, and act like I'm happy?

I've decided to celebrate my birthday. With my last few kopecks, which I'll certainly miss later on, I bought vegetables, wine, sugar, cheese, herring, and so forth. Now I have to clean up, do laundry, iron, cook, and get everything ready. What for? Those around me who will show up are only interested in what's on the table. They make no effort to be cheerful and don't understand me.

Genya will flirt with Yulik again. Afterward Yulik will leave for the front, and I'll remain lonely and poor, without money even for minimal amounts of food, without a roof over my head. What I see ahead of me hurts. I'm already exhausted. Better not think about it now, so I can have a bit of rest!

Thursday the 30th of November [1944]

I cannot sleep. Why? Who woke me up in the middle of the night? A thought has become trapped in my head and can't find its way to freedom. What am I feeling that wants to be expressed? I'm twenty years old now; I have aspirations. I must reach my goal! It's harder for me than last year, because then I still had money and now I don't. Then I had a place to rest my head, and now it's going to be taken away from me. My future and goal are now clearer to me. Now I'm more steadfast and practical in my struggle for existence. I believe in my own strength: I must win—and I will win! I must dedicate myself heart and soul to my studies! The day after tomorrow I'll celebrate my birthday. Yulik will then be completing his studies, before leaving for the army. He is very concerned about me. I believe that a year from now I'll be able to record our meeting after his return. My twenty-first year will be more cheerful!

Monday the 4th of December [1944]

Yesterday I celebrated my birthday. The evening passed joyfully and pleasantly. The red wine created a good mood right away, then the phonograph—and dancing! Yulik was good at amusing the crowd. Naturally, I got some presents: Mayke bought me several books; Lida and Nadia, a box of cookies from the "free market"; Genya, a bottle of perfume and toilet soap. Mayke Tsukarevich, a student at the university who used to be Genya's friend and with whom I've become acquainted, sent me chocolates! I was very, very pleased.

Yulik wants us to get closer before his departure; he's trying to get everything possible out of life, seeking time to enjoy himself. He suggested to me that I stay away from the university for a day in order to spend it with him. I need to explain to him seriously that I dare not do it, that I must study seriously!

Tuesday the 5th of December [1944]

I am preparing for the oral exercises in German grammar. But I'm still waiting for Yulik so that I can say good-bye to him. It is already nine in the evening and he's not here yet. Will he come? Genya told me that they were supposed to meet at the library at ten o'clock this morning so he could return certain materials that he had borrowed from her. She tells me that he didn't come. Maybe they agreed to meet this evening? I'm very sad now. When will we say good-bye?

Monday the 18th of December [1944]

Yulik apologized for not having come over on the fifth. He declared that he loves me, and sees in me a comrade for life, with whom he wants to share his fate. He is older than me, and told me that I'm childishly naïve and not flirtatious. But he figures that when he returns after the war, by then I can be—Lenochka, his wife! He's making serious plans for our future! I am truly still a silly child. I'm not thinking about a husband for the time being. He already needs a wife! Meanwhile, I am different from all the rest. Have I stood still in my development? Yet I love him so much! It seems to me that it is because we are united by a common past, because he is so sensitive and good to me, because he is serious and honest! His tenderness makes me happy.

Yesterday we organized an evening for Samuil Markovich at Genya's. Only I, Yulik, Genya, Lyonya, and Samuil Markovich were there. Yulik behaved very well, did everything to please me. We danced the whole time; he gave me all his attention! Samuil Markovich is of the opinion that I'm lucky that such an "admirable, fine young man loves me." He gave me his blessing. I told him that it's still too early!

Tuesday the 26th of December [1944]

Soon it will be New Year's. Everyone is getting ready to greet the new year, which is supposed to bring joy, good fortune, and peace to humanity. It's possible that I'll be engulfed in the general stream of my surroundings. Meanwhile, I feel bad inside. My financial situation is very strained, and for the time being I can't help myself. Most important of all, I'm left without a roof over my head. I'm still living in the communal apartment, although I no longer have the right to be there. Every month, when the food-ration cards have to be stamped, I rack my brains: how can I trick the administration? For example, my [internal] passport has been held as security for the last five days, until I can provide a document proving that I'm a student at the Bauman Institute. Naturally, I cannot get such a document. What should I do?

Second, New Year's is coming. I have to get together with the old bunch to greet the new year. Despite the fact that I shouldn't leave my room, still I cannot refuse! I need to contribute some money. In my purse I have 100 rubles, which I need for the main meal at the university dining hall! That's all that I can afford. I can't even buy potatoes anymore to cook in the evening. Yet around me there are people who eat normal amounts of good food and dress decently.

In Moscow you can now get a lot of food, fruits, even milk, and all the luxury fabrics for dresses, coats, shoes, boots! I want to dress well like everyone else. Do I have less of a right than other people to happiness? My low shoes are already old, and my dress as well. Samuil Markovich brought me a maroon suit (from the American donations). In order to wear it, it has to be tailored a bit, and for that I need money! In addition, he brought me gray wool for a sweater. For that I also need money!

Yulik is also badly nourished; he is anemic and weak. His blood hemoglobin count is only 58 percent. Normal is 70 percent; in my blood it's 65 percent. That pains me greatly. I feel a lot for him; I don't think about myself, only about him! Things are so hard for both of us, and we cannot help each other. Our unhappy circumstances prevent us from living, from enjoying our good fortune. There's no prospect of anything joyous for us in the near future. Rather, there are stubborn rumors that scholarships will soon be abolished and that attendance at classes will be made optional. This means that I'll absolutely have to work in order to provide the minimum necessities for existence!

The struggle for this little life of mine has become more intense. Of passion and struggle, faith, will, and energy, I have plenty. But will I also have enough strength? Yes, I have serious financial worries, troubling problems, and issues. I have no one to turn to for advice, no one who can help me. I have to do everything and decide everything myself. It will soon be New Year's. Along with everyone else, I have to raise a glass for the new year.

Monday the 15th of January [1945]

Life is rich in experience, events, joy, luck—all mixed up together! Life is engulfing me, and I don't have a minute left to look into my diary. There's simply no time left.

First of all, the semester at the university! After I'd been so ill, I missed more than half the lectures, and the rest of the time was more involved in rhapsodic personal experiences than in studying. For now, everything is fine. I work a lot and need to work even more. I hope that I'll succeed. Everyday I stay a long time in the reading room at the university or in the Lenin Library, and I read, make abstracts, study. Yulik succeeded in getting a furlough to go to Grodno to see his father. He's happy and has already left.

For me it's better that way. For the time being I can calmly prepare for my exams. Though I miss him, I must, after all, think about my duties, and I want to fulfill them.

Something interesting happened again recently, and it made a big impression on me: I got a letter from Yulik's father, my teacher from back home. He called me "daughter" and expressed his wish that I marry Yulik!

I still have studying to do, and Yulik is leaving soon for the front, so for the time being we cannot be joined. For now, I have to struggle for my existence, because once again I am without a kopeck to my name, living in the dorm at the Bauman Institute. I must study a lot and I eat very badly, because I used up all my reserves early. And I always prepared food for Yulik when he came over, because he was hungry, too.

Now it's already the eighteenth, and my dining-hall cards will be good only for two more days. What will happen later? I need money to buy a card at the dining hall. I got a ration card for dried foods for February, so I could make something for Yulik when he visits. But what will I eat during the period of my most stressful work?

Oh, what a calamity!

Friday the 26th of January [1945]

I just got back from a party with a group of young people from Building 10. Three students I know, who are originally from Poland, organized an evening in honor of the liberation of our hometowns. The cognac is still buzzing in my head, but I feel lonely. I miss Yulik! It's two weeks now that he's been gone. I wish he and I were together already.

Monday the 29th of January [1945]

The most stressful time of the first semester at the university. So far, everything is fine. The most important exams will be taking place soon. My mood is good, industrious. Officially, I've been a student at the university for four months. But because of my illness I've attended classes for only two months, and in that time I've developed a feel for the subject matter. I limited myself to enrolling in classes where I attended the lectures, completed the written assignments in German and Latin, and partially prepared for the seminar in Marxism-Leninism, although now that is a distant goal. I think that this semester will be a good start for me. I will study seriously, not only to get an "Excellent," but because I have a feel for the subject. My mind connects the fine threads in my thoughts and reflects upon them.

My love for Yulik still burns brightly and boiling hot. What do his words mean about a future life together, what does his father's proposal mean? Actually, it's what I strive for, but it's still not real. First of all, we are still at war and he's leaving soon for the front. He also dreams of continuing his studies. He's already twenty-four years old. He'll return perhaps a year from now, or in two years! At that age, can you go to school and be supported by your father? Can we then contemplate an independent family life? Either way, I have to carry the heavy burden of supporting my existence. I've received no financial assistance yet, nor do I foresee any. Up to now I slaved away by myself. Now I slave away to put aside something so I can give him a bit of pleasure, because he's everything in the world to me! But as for my studies, where my intellectual development is concerned, he must never hinder me in that! I must get more of a grip on myself, master my emotions, and act not like a frivolous, spoiled child but like an adult. Hasn't life tossed me on stormy waves, on cliffs and abysses? The struggle for entry into the university, the wretched housing in communal rooms, the constant lack of money, the feelings of hunger and poverty—on top of all that, the severe illness following the accident. All this has masked my feelings. it's better that I was blind during such difficult moments. In medical terminology, it is called "a strong narcosis." But now, enough of that. I've avoided some of the dangers. Now I must become healthy. Only I, myself, know how far I deviated from my main axis, how far I strayed. Now—back, back to the straight path! The sooner, the better! Because I have to catch up, reclaim what I've lost, see results.

Monday the 5th of February [1945], 7:00 in the evening

My heart is heavy, very heavy. It's perhaps interesting to constantly struggle, to hurry, to storm barriers that arise repeatedly on the road. Certainly there's quite a lot of poetry in the feelings of suffering. A prickly crown of thorns on one's head is very original and aesthetic, but . . . is it not a means of calming and deceiving oneself, of consoling oneself and becoming satisfied with a gray, tedious, difficult reality? Where is my joy? Do I not have the right, like everyone else, to some rest and to a normal way of life? I, too, want to eat like everyone else! To dress well, not to have such heavy, depressing worries, to afford to go to the theater, and the like.

I read my last words and blush. I've never spoken with anyone about these matters, and I've never complained to anyone either. On the contrary, I hide them from everybody's eyes. For the first time I see my thoughts on paper, and I have this fear inside me that they are no longer my own. Yes, but I cannot stop thinking, I cannot hide and suppress my thoughts and feelings. Always worried about my belly, which can rarely be fooled, I tremble for my corner of my "home," worry about every kopeck, about every rag that you call clothing.

Today is the fifth day of the month, and I'm living on potatoes, salt, bread, and water. In addition, it's now the winter session and I have to work a lot. So I study twelve hours a day and feel my strength giving out. It's true that soon I'll get food on my ration cards, but that will undoubtedly be enough for ten to fifteen days at most! And then, where will I get the money to buy food? To buy potatoes and other trifles?

Here lie the wool and the maroon suit that Samuil Markovich brought me, and I have no money to make anything out of them. I have nothing to wear. To go to the theater you not only have to have money for the ticket (a quarter of the scholarship that's supposed to last for everything for a month), but you also need to have something to wear. Where do I get a dress, shoes, a coat, and so on? I usually pretend that I don't notice my poverty, that my appearance means little to me. But is my aesthetic sensitivity less developed than anyone else's? Am I not just as much a girl who likes to dress tastefully and perhaps even feel more coquettish and feminine?

Up to now (and perhaps beyond) I hoped, deceived myself, that I, too, could have some festive moments, that I, too, could find some rest. But do I not see the reality? Like the ox in the yoke, always in harness. Days in class, then stabs of worry and cramps in my stomach. Soon—in two weeks—the semester will end, and once again I'll have to think about how to get my food-ration cards stamped for the next month, and then I have to start struggling to find a place to live. Where will I find the money?

How long will this torture go on? How long? What can I do to improve my situation? What is my recourse? All around me is a gray sea of pain and worry. Above me, a cold, encroaching sky overcast with thick black clouds. Not one ray of light, not one spark of hope. Eternal, eternal, wanderer and beggar!

Saturday the 10th of February [1945], 6:00 in the evening

It's hard to endure poverty, hard to struggle, but even harder to disappoint yourself. It's hard and painful to lose faith in your own powers, to lose your own self-respect. Sometimes you dream—colorful soap bubbles [part of entry missing] in your fantasy, marble castles in the air built by your sickly faith [part of entry missing], and it seems that it's easier to struggle, that a goal [part of entry missing] is near. And treacherous hopes deceive as always, and suddenly, a terrible shove from reality shatters the whole creation, a psychological earthquake. And it feels like the ground is giving way under your feet, that you're dizzy and feel like crying.

I wander, I seek. I think that I'm striving. I struggle. The least trifle creates problems. Constant difficulties. Still, I believe in myself. Or rather, I did until now. I believed in my abilities. (Why did people praise me, why did they deceive me?) I believed in my will, in my future. Until—I became disappointed in myself, bitterly, grievously disappointed!

It's now the exam period. One exam—History of Antiquity—I passed with "Good," and today the History of Classical Literature with "Satisfactory." These are the results of a half year of study at the university. Is this how I imagined my university studies? Where are those hidden dreams about deep, serious study, how I would bring back the good old days of my outstanding reputation? It is true that in my short period of study I was ill a lot, missed classes. I worked little because of my stormy first love. But are these the only reasons? Can I calmly say that this won't be repeated, that I'm done with this and begin anew?

I know that during the year I'll once again do nothing because I must look for work in order to earn enough for the barest necessities.

And apart from that, as soon as I finish the first session I have to think about my financial worries. I have to start worrying about a place to live and about where to find money. I have all of one ruble in my pocket and have to buy potatoes and bread for daily use; I need change for the streetcar and similar items of daily necessity. But I won't get my scholarship money until the end of the month! All the funds I had up to now are exhausted, and so I have to go to work. Yes, that's very clear. Where and how I'll arrange this I don't yet know, but this will certainly be a concern over the holiday, or I simply won't be able to exist at all!

What will happen to my studies? All my dreams, all my plans are vanishing like intoxicating opium fumes. Farewell! I feel that I've lost the battle, that my exertions are in vain. How ridiculous I look in my own eyes! The one comical thing is the fact that I believed in myself, in my future. Abilities! How foolish. With only average abilities like mine, can you achieve anything without strenuous, systematic work? No! You have to work seriously, rigorously, systematically, diligently. Up to now I haven't done that. Certainly there were objective reasons for it, but it is also my fault to a great extent.

You must not lose your head too much, even when you are very much in love. I lost my head, and I lacked the will to overcome my weakness. In his presence and in his absence, it makes no difference, I still think [*part of entry missing*] about him, summon up his image in my thoughts, long for him. Even now, during the exam period, when every minute counts, I have to struggle with myself for hours in order to keep my mind on my studies and not think about him and his return. Why am I so weak? Am I really such an idle creature? Have I no drop of will left? I am depressed, almost despairing. How hard!

Wednesday the 14th of February [1945], 11:00 at night

Days go by. I'm preparing for the last examination. My standard of living is abnormal as usual. I eat at seven thirty in the morning and then at eight or nine in the evening. All day long I sit in the reading room of the Lenin Library. I study. I struggle with myself and with my own thoughts. Once again—him. Didn't I decide to drive him from my thoughts? Why is he so firmly and deeply rooted in my mind? For fourteen days I've been tortured with anticipation. Every evening my heart trembles with every knock on the door, with every tread of a man's boot. For fourteen days his image has been torturing me and not letting me study. What has he done to deserve it? He always responds coldly to my warm reception and attentions. I never hear a sensitive, attentive word; once in a while a burst of passion, which arouses in me an even greater one, poisoning my last bit of reason. Then, his frivolous and "playful" behavior toward every girl, even in my presence, in my room, which infuriates me. What do I get for my senseless love? For my madness, which has had as its victim my studies and all the naïve childish dreams that had given me strength? Certainly he treats me well. Certainly we are good friends. But that doesn't mean I have no right to satisfy my passion. But I also have no right to sacrifice my studies!

So, yet again, I make resolutions. In vain!

Here I am sitting in a reading room. There are only two days left until the exam. There's still a lot of material to cover. I have to hurry. And suddenly a thought arises—him! I drive it away, I make every effort to pay attention, to grasp the theory of aesthetics and art. Again an image: we are lying together, he embraces me, kisses me, crushes me to his breast. I feel hot, my lips feel dry. I want to run away from myself. What shall I do? Desperately and doggedly I return to Plekhanov's[*] works. I don't understand a single word.

He arrives, tells me of his conversation with his father about me, then he makes a final serious proposal. I prepare a peaceful supper for him and put on the table everything that I have (in reality) been saving for him for a long time. I am seized with furious anger at myself, at him, at the whole world. I'm sunk in foolish dreams at a time when I need to study! What can I be thinking? I'm weak, completely shattered. Why doesn't he come? Let him come, and I will

[*]Georgi Plekhanov (1857–1918): revolutionary theorist, founder of Russian Marxism.

calm down. I'll even greet him coldly, I don't even love him the way I did at first. On the contrary, I hate him now, because he has caused me so much pain; because it's his fault that I'm not studying properly. And yet, I think about him constantly, ceaselessly, without interruption.

Sunday the 18th of February [1945], 12:30 in the afternoon

Yesterday I "earned" my last "Satisfactory." Today I'm already on vacation. The first semester is now behind me. I am immensely dissatisfied. One "Good" and two "Satisfactorys"! When did I ever receive such grades? When was I ever at the bottom of my class? And the most important thing, why?

I've just received a postcard from Grodno. A few words written in haste, which let me know that he'll come at the end of February, possibly after the vacation. And nothing more.

I feel empty and desolate in my soul. I have many practical things to think about. I have to arrange my daily life again, but I don't have the spirit for it. I'd like to fall asleep, to forget everything. He wishes me great success in my exams. A bit late for that, isn't it? It will be interesting to see how he reacts. He'll certainly be disappointed. It's all the same to me. Let him think whatever he wants, let him do whatever he wants. He can love me or not. I am a hollowed-out oak.

Wednesday the 28th of February [1945], 2:00 in the afternoon

Now my heart is still, almost still. The oppressive stillness after a storm. The last bit of wind tugs at a random leaf left on a bare tree, the last raindrops drip, but, as one can easily predict, a deathly stillness soon will reign. Shh, still as a cemetery.

A revolution in my life in the course of seven days. Seven vacation days that were the equivalent of seven whole years. "He" arrived. In a friendly and courteous manner he told me about his trip, about his impressions. Then he went so far as to hug and kiss me. The same evening he boldly flirted with Tamara, who behaved provocatively. In a word, a continuation of the previous situation, but I was more aware of it because I had placed so many hopes on his return, because after his absence—after the pain of my longing, after my distress about the sad outcome of the semester, after financial woes—I longed for understanding, warmth, attentiveness, sympathy. Yes. Suddenly the veil dropped from my eyes and I saw daylight! A rosy dream that I lived with for five months has burst like a soap bubble. Reality revealed itself in all its brutal nakedness.

For what, for whom, did I wreck my plans for the future with my own hands? Where have my aspirations gone, the will to work? I sacrificed everything for him. He didn't appreciate it and flirted left and right. Maybe it's not his fault, and I do not blame him. He's just an ordinary, insensitive person, who has unappealing attitudes toward life. I myself don't know how it happened that fate caused our paths to cross for a while. In my fantasy, my hunger for happiness, a bright dream flickered, obscuring my view of reality. Now it's all become clear to me. It was hard for me to part with my dream, much harder than to part with him. Perhaps because the dream was my happiness: And is it possible to take one's leave of happiness? But I understood the need to break it off.

My courteous, sincere, short letter, instead of going to the theater with him. He went with Tamara and came back to spend the night with her. Or so it would seem, because he saw her home. Even earlier, he left me a letter in which he responds very politely, warmly, tactfully. He had brought me several trifles from Grodno, presents from his father and himself. In general, he behaves tactfully in my presence and very differently in Genya's company—as Genya tells it, which I can believe only up to a point, because she's very pleased with the situation and is strongly inclined to flirt. He suggested getting together with Genya, and she is very pleased.

The first couple of days were very, very hard for me. Now it is a lot easier. I seem to be indifferent to him. I think very little about him altogether. Tomorrow the second semester is starting. Again I go to the university every day, but how different it is from before! Before, I used to go because it was my duty. During lectures I often thought about him and daydreamed about whether he would come over in the evening. Now it is easier. Tomorrow I'm going to the university with my mind clear. Only now do I recall the enthusiasm with which I arrived at the university, the plans I had. I blush. How could I have forgotten all that? I remember the letter that Irina Vasilievna wrote me: she predicts success for me wherever my work, endurance, and will take me. How deceived she was! But more than anyone I deceived myself. I don't regret the past, because I was happy and I loved. But I lost a lot, a lot. And because my precious and stormy love affair now belongs to the past, I must make up for lost time and study, study hard. During the past semester, I had the opportunity to realize how interesting and profound everything is in my courses; now I need only to be principled in my decisions and carry out what I have decided.

I'm overcome with depression and have to summon my last vestiges of strength in order to maintain my equilibrium. A lotus leaf would help more than anything else. Although there's really no serious need for that now. Gradually everything will be forgotten. My surroundings once again will take on their familiar appearance. Every object will regain its normal shape and color, and things will be called by their real names.

Monday the 5th of March [1945], 8:00 in the evening

I was cursed (and perhaps blessed, who knows?) from the day of my birth. Never any rest, not one minute of psychological equilibrium. Constant inner struggle, opposing forces constantly tearing my soul in two. Now as well, perhaps more than ever. Is there not enough gall in my last bitter glass? Or haven't I yet drunk the poison down to the last drop?

Is it so easy to bear the burden of a deep morass in my soul, the burden of depression? Yet, that's what I need most in order to rest a bit and gather my strength. I want to forget, forget entirely: Is that so easy? But fate has denied me even that. "He" will not leave me alone. What more does he want from me? Now he has taken to visiting, to writing letters, in which he writes that he's unworthy of my love, that I am an angel, and the like. Begs me at least to be his friend. Why? What does he mean by it? Why does he need me, since, as he himself admitted, he never loved me, only rationally calculated that he could be happy with me? He even told Genya that he tried to convince himself that he loved me, but he didn't succeed. What does he want now? I have given him a free hand. What more does he need? Certainly his ego and pride are hurt: I, a twenty-year-old, inexperienced girl, of whom he was so sure, has turned him down. Is that the only reason he's trying so hard to get me back? Oh, his behavior is so base! And perhaps he feels some responsibility for his emotional outpourings? And, as he puts it himself, he wants me to understand that he always behaved honestly. Oh, that ego again! He wants to exit with a clear conscience. But I have never blamed him. Let him leave me alone.

Saturday the 14th of April [1945], 10:00 in the evening

How long haven't I looked into my diary! More than a month already. Much water has flowed under the bridge since then. Yulik left for the front. Before his departure we said good-bye coldly, even more than coldly. At the party we arranged at his suggestion, he flirted with Tamara and in general behaved strangely. Now he is half-forgotten. Half, because at times he creeps into my thoughts all the same. How weak and foolish I am.

My heart is empty and bleak. My life is very, very bad, in material terms. I go hungry quite often, and don't even have enough money for the midday meal. Debts, debts. I do study, but only at a slow pace, because I lack the strength; I want something to eat, and I fall asleep. A lot of time is wasted on empty dreaming. At the university my oral report was a big success. At first I felt good about it, but now it's all the same to me. Regardless, I will never achieve anything under these circumstances. What will be will be.

I've started to flirt with Oleg.

Tuesday the 24th of April [1945], 8:00 in the evening

Anxiety is tearing apart my soul. I want something, but I myself don't know what. I understand that I have to work, but I do nothing. That creates dissatisfaction. Still, I continue to do nothing. Last week I was sick. Everyone says that I look very bad, and actually I feel very weak. The worst is that I am very, very negligent, altogether disorganized. Days go by haphazardly, without a plan, with everything happening haphazardly and sometimes nothing happening at all. How can I explain such negligence, indifference to everything in the world? Again dreams, empty dreams about the future, again him, and reminiscence about the recent past. But that is now *mezhdu prochim* [Russian: by the way]. I don't much care, because I'm indifferent to everything, even the recent past. It is hard to live without a purpose! And that is how I live now. I jump from place to place. For instance, what did I do today? I got up at eight o'clock. Genya spent the night here. I washed the floor, cleaned the room, and at eleven o'clock I left for the university. I stayed for only one of the two hours of Hygiene.

Then to the dining hall. Stood in line for my stipend. Read a bit, very little, of Dante's *Divine Comedy*. Suddenly I felt I wanted to go home. I came home. Suddenly it occurred to me to make pancakes. I started cooking, then stopped, because I was sick of pancakes (though I do want to eat). Now, apparently, I'll go to sleep, though I absolutely do not want to. What should I do? How can I find a way to get organized? What should I do with myself? I am so weak—physically and, even more so, psychologically—lacking the financial means to live, negligent, without a goal, dreamily falling apart.

Saturday the 19th of May [1945], 11:30 at night

It's peacetime again. Where in my diary are the echoes of the thirty salvos from the one thousand artillery pieces? Where is the shadow of the brilliant bouquets of fireworks that shot up so rapidly and descended even more speedily? Where is the trace of merriment, joy? The war is over. Soon, very soon, families will be reunited, people will get back what the war took away from them. And for me? Peace brings me nothing of all that the war took away.

Again, lack of money, in debt over my head. Soon, in a month, the semester begins. I'm badly prepared; how I'll pass I really don't know. Naturally I'm working now, but not productively, because I feel unwell physically. I believe that I've lost a great deal of strength because of the bad food I eat. It doesn't matter to me how I pass, as long as I somehow pass, so I can get my stipend. In any case, I've long been convinced that I'll never be a good student. First of all, because I am not used to working seriously, and second, because under these circumstances I cannot study productively. *"Byte opredelyayet soznanie."* [Russian: "Being determines consciousness."]

Next year I will definitely work.

How foolish! My foolish heart waits impatiently for a letter, and the letter doesn't come. Why am I waiting at all? Isn't everything over? Did I not end it myself? Did I lack the facts to prove to myself that I shouldn't regret my action? And yet I tremble every evening when I go home in anticipation of a letter. No. I know for sure: I must end it, tear it out by the roots. How deeply he is implanted! I didn't know it myself before.

Tuesday the 24th of July [1945], 10:00 in the morning

Behind me is the first academic year at Moscow University. The results were far from satisfactory: two "Excellents," two "Goods," one "Satisfactory." But that's not what is most important. The most important thing is actually the fact that I didn't take my studies seriously. Every other day I came up with new theories about how this isn't the most important thing in life, that I'm young and have to enjoy life, and so on. But I was only deceiving myself, because in any case I have no opportunities to enjoy life or even just to live decently, and all my "theories" were just a mask to cover my despair, my bad mood. And what do I see now? The year has gone by idle, empty. I wandered erratically. Now I am free and there's time to think, to review my situation. What now? *Coz dalej, szary czlowieku*? [Polish "What now, gray man?"]

What's the point of studying if I learn nothing and then end up working in Siberia or in the middle of nowhere? Have I lost my earlier interest in literature, languages, and the like? To be sure, my circumstances are not the easiest, but that doesn't give me the right to behave so frivolously! Can I no longer aspire? Can I really not compete? Have I really lost my pride and allowed everyone else to be better than me?

I strayed for a year. What have all my theories brought me? Pleasure, joy, happiness? After the sad end of my first love, all the "theories" began to bloom (out of despair, I believe), but no trace is left of them now. Empty and vacant. Nothing left. So from what shall I live? How shall I spend my time? And once again I repeat the words from last year: *"Budushchei god, vse eto popravit."* [Russian: "Next year, all this will be set right."]

But will it really? I've already lost trust in myself. As it turns out, I am very, very weak. Has life really broken me so early?

I'm preparing to go to Karakulino for a rest. There I'll have a lot of time and few cares, so perhaps I'll be able to come up with something.

ᑉᣚᕲ

Later entry — date unclear; possibly, the 28th of August [1945], 10:00 in the morning

So that I wouldn't have to remain alone in the dorm in such poor circumstances, my dear friend Mayke took me home with her to Ukraine. They now live in the town of Niezhin, where her parents are professors at the university. Before the war they lived in Kiev, but during the war they stayed in Ilovutka, not far from Stalingrad. When they returned to Kiev, their apartment was already occupied.

But this apartment is also very nice. In this town you can get a lot of good food, even fruit. I brought my bread-and food-ration cards and gave them to Mayke. Her mother now makes wonderful meals for us!

Mayke had already told her parents about my origins, the death of my family, even my recent accident, so they treat me very warmly! They have paid me many compliments for my knowledge of Yiddish, because in the years following the Revolution they were teachers in the Yiddish schools! Unfortunately, the Yiddish schools were closed in 1936, which they very much regret. Now they are teachers in Ukrainian and Russian schools. The father is a professor of mathematics; the mother, of history. Since there is still a Yiddish cultural organization in Kiev, created by the former Yiddish writers and teachers, they even convinced Mayke that we should visit this organization. So, off we went to Kiev, and Mayke showed me the city: a beautiful city with many houses, beautiful gardens, and woods. It is here that the famous Jewish military leader[*] who defeated the German army at Kuybyshev has settled.

At the Jewish cultural organization they admired my Yiddish, because few young people of my age now can speak like me or even know Yiddish literature. They even suggested that I read Sholem Asch's latest work, *The Nazarene*, which was recently published. They gave me the book. I read it and was taken aback: What was it about the character of Jesus that interested Sholem Asch? He wanted to be the Messiah and to have the destiny of God.[†]

---

[*] It is not clear who is meant here.

[†] Sholem Asch (1880–1957) was a Yiddish novelist and dramatist. When he wrote novels on Jesus and Mary, he was attacked by much of the Yiddish press, which viewed his work as encouraging conversion to Christianity, leaving him alienated from Jewish cultural life.

Epilogue: Lena's Life after the Diary Ends

While a university student in Moscow, Lena worked as a translator for the office of the Polish embassy responsible for locating Polish citizens who had been sent to Soviet labor camps during the war. Knowing that none of her own relatives were alive, Lena had not attempted to go back to Poland. In the autumn of 1947, however, there began a wave of attacks directed against the works—and ultimately the lives—of Jewish writers, intellectuals, and political leaders in the Soviet Union. One of the first victims was Isaac Nusinov, who had been Lena's Russian literature professor at the university. Lena decided to return to Poland, where her friend Genya lived. She was one year short of a master's degree in foreign languages and literature.

On September 17, 1947, Lena arrived in Lodz, Poland, where she began to attend the University of Lodz. A short while later, Genya introduced her to a friend, Sholem Rozenberg. Sholem was searching for his brother Ksyl, who had been sent to a Soviet labor camp during the war. Lena used her contacts in the Polish embassy in Moscow to help track down Ksyl. During that time, she and Sholem grew closer, united by a common bond of dedication to Yiddish language and culture. On December 27, 1947, they were married. Sholem's brother was liberated on May 15, 1948, and Lena and Sholem went to Warsaw to join Ksyl upon his release.

Sholem and Ksyl were active in the Jewish socialist labor movement, the Bund. But the political mood in Poland hardened, and the Bund was under pressure to merge into the Communist Party. In August 1948, Ksyl, Sholem, and Lena (now six months pregnant) fled Poland. Crossing illegally into Czechoslovakia and later

Germany, they finally arrived in Paris on September 22, 1948. Two months later, Lena's son was born.

The first immigrant years were very hard. First Lena and then Sholem spent long periods in a sanatorium battling tuberculosis. Lena was isolated there from January 19, 1950, until the end of that year, and suffered its aftereffects for three years. Sholem was in the sanatorium from November 1952 until the end of 1953. When able to work, Lena helped Sholem in his tailor shop in Paris. The shop was successful, and gradually their situation improved. They subsequently had two daughters.

Lena was very active in Yiddish cultural life in Paris, often reciting Yiddish poetry at the Medem library and cultural center, Europe's largest repository of Yiddish literature. She made Yiddish-language learning tapes with Professor Yitzkhok Niborski—who wrote the preface to the Yiddish version of this book—and occasionally contributed literary reviews to the Paris Yiddish newspapers.

Some forty years after her departure from Russia, Lena went back for a visit. As she matured, Lena had gradually come to realize the extent to which Samuil Markovich, with whom she had clashed so bitterly during her years at the children's home, had been responsible for her survival and that of the other children. She had a warm reunion with him and Berta Pavlovna in Leningrad, as well as with several of her former classmates. Lena had also stayed in touch with other friends from the children's home, many of whom had moved to Israel or the United States. Genya became a professor of Russian at the University of California. She died in 1998. Samuil Markovich died in 1999. Berta Pavlovna, age one hundred and four, lives in Brooklyn.

Toward the end of the 1980s, Lena began exhibiting signs of a degenerative neurological illness. As her memory faded, she struggled to transcribe her diary from its original notebooks into publishable form. When she was unable to complete the diary project, Sholem took over and arranged for publication of the original Yiddish version in Paris in 1999. Today, Lena lives at home in Paris, cared for by her husband. This book attests to a history that she can no longer recount.

Lena, Moscow 1946